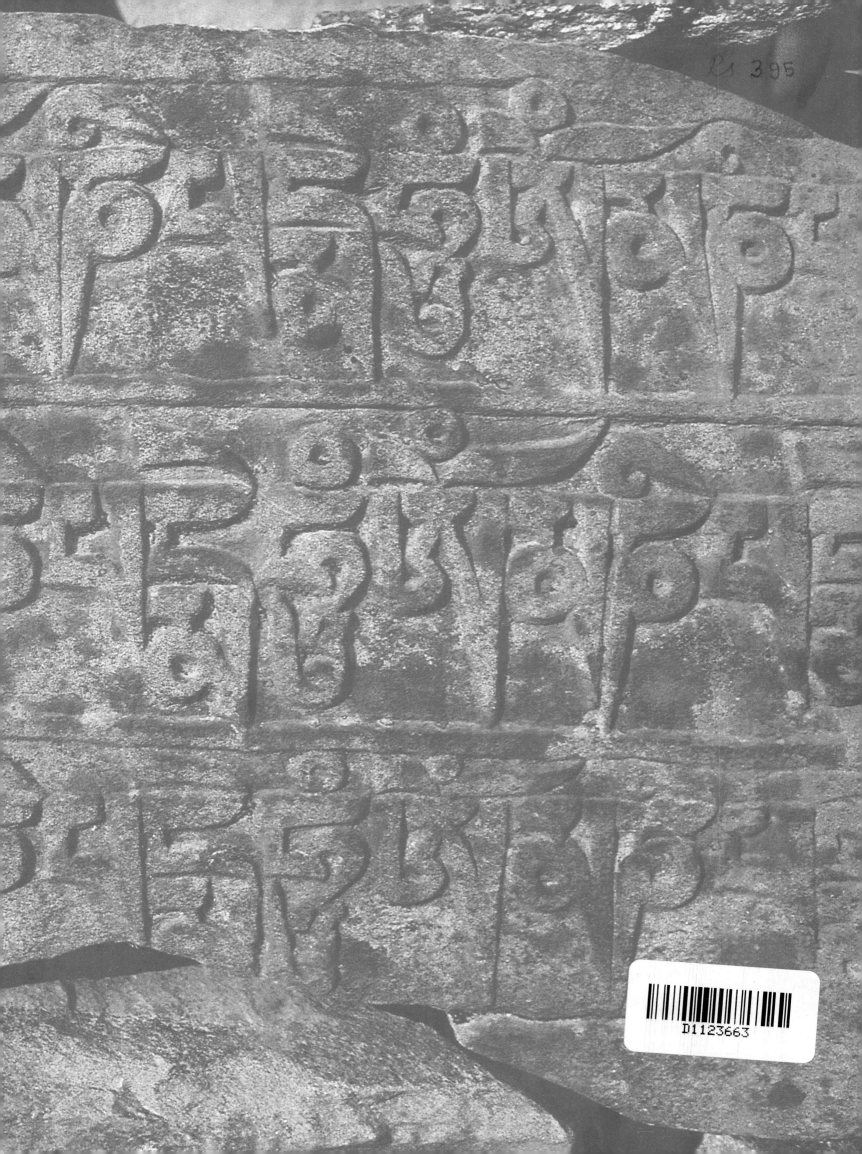

NEPAL

Journey through
NEPAL

Mohamed Amin · Duncan Willetts
Brian Tetley

THE BODLEY HEAD
LONDON

Acknowledgements

We would like to thank the many people in Nepal who gave us help and advice in preparing this book. We are particularly grateful to Mike Blackall of Sheraton Hotels, the management and staff at Everest Sheraton, including Dubby Bhagat, and William Maa and his colleagues of Lama Excursions and Gaida Wildlife Camp. Our thanks also to Rajendra Sharma and Arun Pokharel — and, of course, to all the people of Nepal who made us so welcome.

First published 1987 by
The Bodley Head Ltd,
32 Bedford Square,
London WCIB 3 EL

© Camerapix 1987

British Library Cataloguing in Publication Data
Amin, Mohamed
      Journey through Nepal
      1. Nepal — Description and travel
      I. Title   II. Willetts, Duncan
      III. Tetley, Brian
      915.49' 604   DS 493.53

ISBN   0 370 31096 9

This book was designed and produced by
Camerapix Publishers International,
P.O. Box 45048,
Nairobi, Kenya

Design: Craig Dodd

Half-title: Laughing Newar weaver girls; Monkey temple at Swayambunath, Kathmandu; celebrants at religious festival. Title page: Sacred mountain, Machhapuchhare; wild peacock, Royal Chitwan National Park; River running on the Trisuli; Suikhet Valley women on mountain trail. Contents Page: Asiatic rhino with calf; Kathmandu's Living Goddess.

Following pages: Massive ramparts of rock and ice guard southern approaches to Sagamartha, 'Goddess of the Universe', 29,028 foot high Everest, including jagged ridges of 27,890 foot high Lhotse at right. The Royal Nepal Airlines flight at 20,000 feet along the outer edge of this sea of mountains is one of the most dramatic and awe-inspiring in the world.

Contents

1. Introduction:
Journey through Nepal

Spawned high in a valley between two nameless 20,000 foot Tibetan peaks the waters of Nepal's Trisuli River begin as a trickle of ice melt, a tiny babbling brook. Yet in less than 160 kilometres, its raging waters joined and swollen by the torrents of a dozen feeders to cut deep gorges through the mightiest mountain range in the world, the Himalaya, this river plunges from 17,000 feet to just above sea level. The mountain slopes, down which it leaps and bounds on its journey to the sea, run east to west along Nepal's entire 885 kilometre long northern border with Tibet. They form a stupendous pedestal which lifts at least a quarter of Nepal's landlocked 141,414 square kilometres more than 10,000 feet above sea level, reaching an apex, the highest point on Planet Earth, at 29,028 feet.

Beyond this daunting massif of rock, which at an average height of 20,000 feet is the 'Roof of the World', the turbulent river joins three other major rivers at the base of the outer, parallel range of the Mahabharat Lekh which rises between 5,000 to 9,000 feet above sea level.

It is beyond here, at the base of this second range of mountains, that the combined torrent, now named the Narayani River, broadens out to cut a wide swathe across the broad flood plains of the Inner Terai and, with majestic serenity, flow through the lush foliage of the Royal Chitwan National Park. During the height of the summer monsoons and ice melt, at full flood, it takes these waters just 12 hours to complete a journey — from Arctic ice to tropical jungle — that begins in the mystic permafrost of the remote, almost impenetrable high country and travel through a world in microcosm.

Such is the complexity and the beauty of Nepal, an ancient and tiny Kingdom little bigger than England and Wales that, through the ages, has lured mystics, philosophers, and adventurers from the time long before the manifestation of all goodness, Lord Buddha, was born within sight and sound of these same flood waters. Like all Nepal's rivers and mountains, the Trisuli's waters have spiritual significance, too, as do the ice peaks above them which sustain their flow.

Not for nothing is the land of 20th century King Birendra Bir Bikram Shah Dev known as the 'Abode of the Gods' for here were nurtured not only the Lord Buddha but the most eminent Hindu deities including Lord Shiva and his consort Parvati. Indeed, Hindus believe the waters of the sacred lake of Gosainkund, from which the Trisuli River draws much of its strength, were formed when Shiva thrust his trident into the mountainside to create three gushing streams.

From the watershed marked by the 23,771 foot high peak of Langtang Lirung, which overlooks the upper reaches of the Trisuli, the pilgrim can gaze across the valley and look upon the nearby twin peaks of sacred Gaurisankar, the north summit of which represents Shiva; its south his consort. Sacred also to Buddhists, especially the Sherpa people of this region of Nepal who call it 'Jomo Tsheringma', Gaurisankar's cliffs and rock escarpments sweep steeply upwards to 23,442 feet. Seen ages ago from the Terai Plains in the south, these peaks gave rise to ancient Nepalese folk legends that it was the highest mountain in the world.

It is the waters born on these slopes which join the Trisuli to sustain the most sacred of all Hindu rivers. For as the Narayani they flow into India to join the Ganges at Hajipur, in India's Bihar State, just

Above: Marble statue of the founder of modern Nepal, King Tribhuvan, who returned from a self-imposed exile in India on February 1951 to overthrow the Rana dynasty and usher his country into the modern world after a century of isolation, stands outside Kathmandu's national sports stadium. He died four years after his return to be succeeded by his son, King Mahendra.

Above: Statue of 18th century King Prithvi Narayan Shah, outside Singh Durbar (Lion Palace) Kathmandu. The Palace built in 1901 is now the Government Secretariat.

downstream from the confluence of the Holy River and its other major tributary, the Ghaghara.

Perhaps Shiva and his consort have found eternal peace here among the wind-blown spindrift snow of their lofty abode. Certainly Gaurisankar did not yield its summits easily. Not until 1979 did an American climber, and a Sherpa born in the mountain's shadow, become the first mortals to set foot atop its highest pinnacle and gaze upon this haven of the most celebrated of Hindu deities.

Many more Gods and Goddesses make their home among the mighty Himalaya. There is Sagarmatha, 'Goddess of the Universe' atop the highest point on earth, 29,028 foot high Everest and Annapurna, 'Goddess of Plenty', atop the lofty peak of 26,545 foot high Annapurna I while Ganesh, the elephant-headed God, lives on top of 24,299 foot high Ganesh Himal.

To most Nepalese, these are not phantoms conjured up out of myth, folklore and superstition but living deities, the most sacred of realities. Today devotion is as great a part of Nepalese life as it ever was; perhaps more so, for whatever faith the people of this happy land follow — be it Hinduism, Buddhism, Tantric or animism — they remain true to their gods and also to their joyous nature. 'We may be poor,' says a typical young Nepali, 'but we're not miserable. When it comes to laughter we've got the highest Gross National Product (GNP) of any country — happiness!'

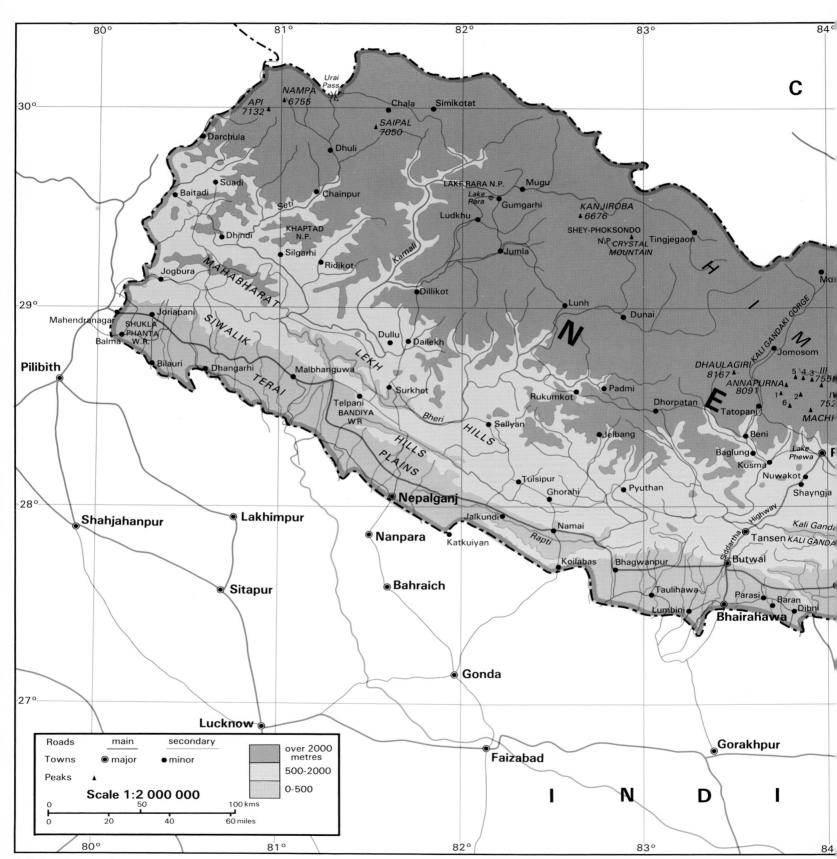

C

80° 81° 82° 83° 84°

30°

Urai Pass

NAMPA ▲6755
API ▲7132
Chala • Simikotat •

SAIPAL 7050
Darchula •
Dhuli •

Suadi •
Baitadi •
LAKE RARA N.P.
Mugu •
Lake Rara
Chainpur •
Gumgarhi •
KANJIROBA ▲6676

Seti
Ludkhu •
SHEY-PHOKSONDO
Dhindi •
KHAPTAD N.P.
Tingjegaon •
N.P. *CRYSTAL MOUNTAIN*

Silgarhi •
Jumla •
Ridikot •

M
u

Jogbura •
Dillikot •
Lunh •

29°
Mahendranagar •
Joriapani •
Dunai •
Kali Gandaki Gorge

SHUKLA PHANTA W.R.
Balma •
Dullu • Dailekh •
N
Jomosom •

Bilauri •
DHAULAGIRI 8167 ▲
5 4 3 III
▲▲▲ 755
Pilibith ⊙
Dhangarhi •
Malbhanguwa •
LEKH
ANNAPURNA 8091
1
▲ ▲2
752

Surkhet •
Rukumkot •
Padmi •
Dhorpatan •
E
6 ▲

Telpani
BANDIYA W R
Bheri
Sallyan •
Jelbang •
Tatopani • MACHH

HILLS
Beni •

TERAI
Baglung •
Lake Phewa

HILLS
Kusma •
PLAINS
Tulsipur •
Ghorahi •
Pyuthan •
Nuwakot •
Shayngja •

28°
Nepalganj ⊙
Jalkundi •
Namai •
Highway
Kali Ganda

Shahjahanpur ⊙
Lakhimpur ⊙
Katkuiyan •
Rapti
Siddartha
Tansen *KALI GANDA*

Nanpara ⊙
Koilabas •
Bhagwanpur •
Butwal ⊙

Sitapur ⊙
Bahraich ⊙
Taulihawa •
Parasi •
Baran •

Lumbini •
Bhairahawa
Dibni

Gonda ⊙

27°

Lucknow ⊙

Roads	main	secondary
Towns	⊙ major	• minor
Peaks	▲	

Gorakhpur ⊙

Faizabad ⊙

	over 2000 metres
	500-2000
	0-500

Scale 1:2 000 000

0   50   100 kms
0   20   40   60 miles

I   N   D   I

80° 81° 82° 83° 84

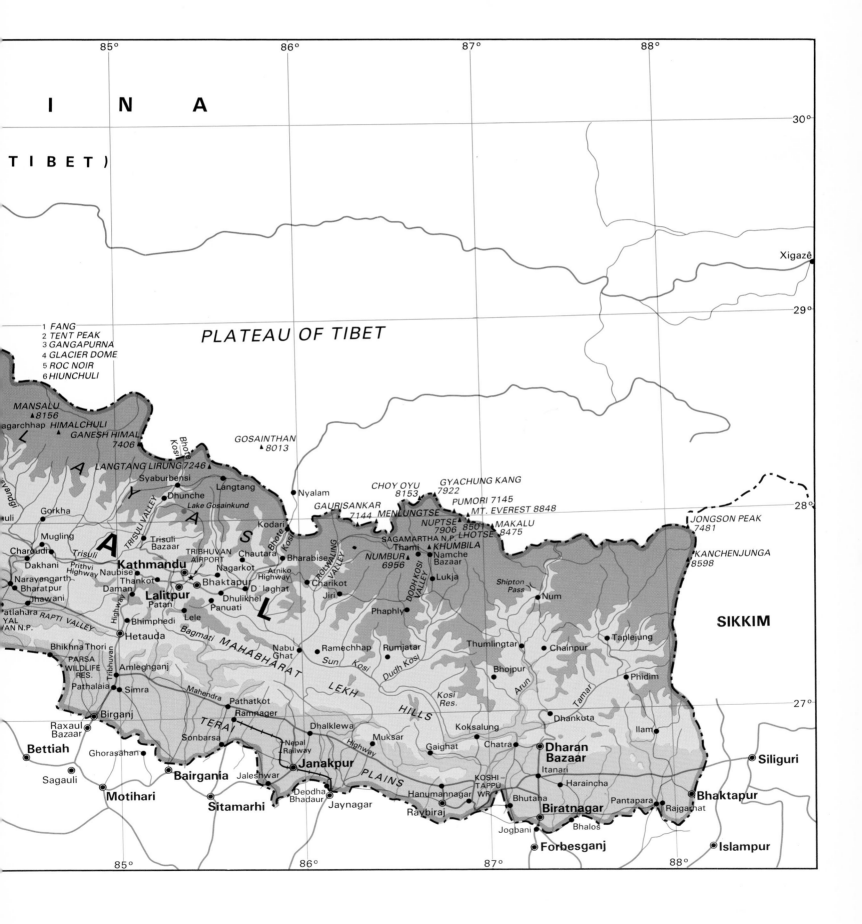

85°　　　　　　86°　　　　　　87°　　　　　　88°

30°

I N A

T I B E T)

29°

1 FANG
2 TENT PEAK
3 GANGAPURNA
4 GLACIER DOME
5 ROC NOIR
6 HIUNCHULI

PLATEAU OF TIBET

Xigazê

MANSALU
▲8156
HIMALCHULI
agarchhap ▲
GANESH HIMAL
7406
Bhote Kosi
GOSAINTHAN
▲8013

LANGTANG LIRUNG 7246▲
Syaburbensi
Langtang

28°

vandi
Gorkha
Dhunche
Lake Gosainkund
Nyalam

CHOY OYU
8153
GYACHUNG KANG
7922
PUMORI 7145
MT. EVEREST 8848

JONGSON PEAK
7481

uli
Mugling
Trisuli
Bazaar

TRISULI VALLEY

Kodari

GAURISANKAR
7144 MENLUNGTSE
NUPTSE
7906 8501
LHOTSE MAKALU
8475

KANCHENJUNGA
8598

Charoudi
Trisuli
Chautara
Bharabise

SAGARMATHA N.P.
Thami
▲KHUMBILA

Dakhani
Prithvi
Highway
Naubise

TRIBHUVAN
AIRPORT
Nagarkot
Arniko
Highway

NUMBUR▲
6956
Namche
Bazaar

Kathmandu
Bhaktapur

Bharabise

Bharatpur
Thankot

D laghat
Charikot
Jiri
Lukja

Shipton
Pass
Num

Narayangarth
Bharatpur
Jhawani
Daman
Lalitpur
Patan
Dhulikhel
Panuati

Phaphly

atlahara
YAL
AN N.P.

RAPTI VALLEY
Bhimphedi
Lele

DODH KOSI VALLEY

CHOLMALING VALLEY

Bagmati

MAHABHARAT

Nabu
Ghat
Ramechhap
Rumjatar

Thumlingtar
Chainpur

SIKKIM

Hetauda

Sun Kosi
Dudh Kosi

Bhojpur

27°

Bhikhna Thori

Tribhuvan Highway

Amleghganj

LEKH

HILLS

Kosi
Res.

Arun

Tamar

Dhankuta

Taplejung

PARSA
WILDLIFE
RES.

Simra

Mahendra

Pathatkot
Ramnager

Phidim

Pathalaia

Birganj

Ilam

Raxaul
Bazaar

Sonbarsa
TERAI

Dhalklewa
Muksar

Koksalung
Gaighat
Chatra

Dharan
Bazaar

Ghorasahan
Nepal
Railway

Highway

Itanari
Haraincha

Siliguri

Bettiah

Sagauli

Bairgania
Jaleshwar

Janakpur

PLAINS

Hanumannagar

KOSHI-
TAPPU WR

Bhutaha

Pantapara

Rajgachat

Bhaktapur

Motihari

Sitamarhi

Deodha
Bhadaur
Jaynagar

Raybiraj

Biratnagar

Bhalos

Jogbani

Forbesganj

Islampur

85°　　　　　　86°　　　　　　87°　　　　　　88°

Above: Swimming pool of the five-star Everest Sheraton, Kathmandu's classiest hotel.

In all the world, there is no other land like this which honours the red rhododendron as its national flower and reveres the cow as sacred. And laid among and along its marvels of plains, mountains and rivers is a tapestry of vivid cultural contrasts — a mosaic of 35 ethnic cultures made up not only of happy folk but brave and hardy ones too, the Gurkha and the Sherpa among them. The 18 million Nepalese people are as diverse and colourful as the serrated landscapes of their rectangularly-shaped nation.

For most visitors, however, the first sight of this incredible kingdom is from the air — a stunning, mind-numbing panorama of jagged and monumental ice-clad peaks that roll away into the distance, peak upon peak, as far as the eye can see. Laid out below the plane is a vista of such grandeur that for many people it will remain etched upon the mind long after most of life's memories have faded and withered.

From the narrow strip of flat, fertile, chequer-board plain which lies at 220 feet above sea level along the Indian border — interspersed by the Siwalik and Churia Hills clad with hardwood forest — Nepal climbs, in a series of integrated steps, ascending foothills, raised valleys, and lateral mountains, nowhere more than 240 kilometres at its widest and under 150 kilometres at its narrowest, to more than 29,000 feet.

The centre of the Himalaya, which stretches in a crescent for almost 2,500 kilometres from India's border with Burma in the east to Pakistan in the west, lies between Nepal and Tibet and contains eight of the world's 10 highest peaks — all above 26,250 feet. Hemmed in between the giant nations of China, India and Pakistan, only slightly larger than the neighbouring kingdom of Bhutan, Nepal is a land of vertical perspective: everything is on the up or viewed above the head.

It gives a new dimension to travel, too. Within the span of 12 hours it is the easiest of arrangements to fly with the rising sun along the daunting

*Right: Traditional Nepalese folk dancing entertains
diners at the Everest Sheraton.*

barrier of the Himalaya and then, disembarking at Kathmandu's
Tribhuvan Airport, drive along the road cut into the side of a deep
Himalayan river gorge and down the precipitous flanks of the
Mahabharat range to the emerald plains of the Terai to ride elephant
among a herd of rhino as the sun sets.

Similarly, the south-north land journey through Nepal, from sea-level
border to mountain fastness, a swift and stunning transformation of
environment, is only a matter of a few hours, starting at the Indian
border after a comfortable breakfast and concluding in the late afternoon
at the Tibetan border, before a comfortable dinner back at base in the
capital of Kathmandu.

The east-west traverse, however, is one of the toughest treks in the
world, only really possible to accomplish on foot and with great difficulty
over many weeks; and still a matter of many days even when tackled on
the horizontal surfaces of the lowland plains as a combination of vehicle
and foot travel.

Even by 1987 there was still no road that crossed the length of Nepal,
although a network of roads built since the 1970s, many carved out of the
sheer walls of the river valleys, now criss-crosses the breadth of the
nation to link the major midland towns and resort areas, as well as the
south-north borders.

All this — the hydro-electric schemes to tap the gushing mountain
torrents, the satellite ground station in the bowl of the Kathmandu
Valley, the roads and the dramatic bridges which leap from one side of a
gorge to another and the expansion at Kathmandu's international airport
— is evidence of the astonishing transformation which is taking place in
this once isolated mountain kingdom.

Above: Newar mother and child outside the elegantly carved door of their Bhaktapur home.

Nepal came late to the family of modern nations. Until 1950 it was virtually a closed and shuttered society: a living antiquity. Indeed, in the 1980s a walk down some of the narrow, cobblestone streets of the ancient cities of the Kathmandu Valley, with their overhanging 'Juliet' balconies and delicately-wrought carved windows, was like taking a stroll back through time — into the Middle Ages of medieval Europe.

And yet, by its own calendar, there is nothing remotely backward about Nepal. Indeed, it may well be the most advanced nation on earth. In April 1986, for instance, hundreds of thousands of celebrants choked the streets of Thimmi, one of the old cities of Kathmandu Valley, to celebrate the dawn of the year 2043!

The ancient capital, seat of the Royal family, fittingly lies squarely at the centre of the country — both in terms of geographical location and altitude.

Set 4,368 foot above sea level, on roughly the same latitude as that of Florida, Kathmandu boasts one of the most perfect climates in the world — neither too hot nor too cold, Summer maximums touch around 30°C and the mean winter temperature is a benevolent 10°C.

Below: Old woman relaxing with a hookah pipe by the banks of the Trisuli River.

Bottom: Shiva worshipping holy man, sadhu, *relaxing at one of Kathmandu's Hindu shrines.*

Though sometimes frosty the season is dry and without snow. Such munificence in matters of weather must have been ordered by the Gods and Nepal justifiably celebrates its divine fortune by harvesting at least three harvests — grains like rice and wheat — a year.

The tree-clad slopes of the Valley walls, which climb from between 6,500 to 7,000 feet, are verdant with stands of oak, alder, rhododendron and jacaranda. The slopes provide unsurpassed views of the northern mountains while the blossoms bestow upon the Nepalese capital a warmth reflected in the faces and the greetings of its residents.

The majority of Kathmandu's citizens belong to the resourceful tribe of the Newar, just one of Nepal's many ethnic groups, who display the brightness of their culture on a multi-coloured ethnic canvas as complex as the landscape.

In the mountains above these temperate valleys, the barren, tundra-like landscapes and the monsoon rains and snow, together with the winter frosts, limit farming. But during the brief festival of summer, in isolated valleys often lush with forest growth and grasses, potatoes are cultivated as high as 13,000 feet and barley even higher. The people who live in these regions, which form a majority of the country's land area, are frugal and hardy like the unyielding land which they till. But they themselves are in the minority.

The majority of the fast-growing population occupies the narrow strip of plains at its southern boundary, and the temperate valleys like Kathmandu that dominate its midlands. Yet despite its fertile valleys Nepal may soon find itself hard pressed to be self-sufficient in food.

Already, over-cultivation of the precipitous valley slopes above the river gorges has turned Nepal into a text-book example of deforestation and soil erosion. The terraces of the abandoned rice paddies eventually crumble and the next monsoon rains can bring literally thousands of tons of mountainside, no longer held together by roots of trees or grasses, crashing down the slopes.

Yet fragile as the surface may be, Nepal's beauty remains virtually indestructible. Seen from the air, even the eroded walls of the valleys retain a magnificence of form and shape that take the breath away.

It is these same mountain walls which kept Nepal remote from the world until this century — and which in many regions, even today, keep the Nepalese remote from each other. Some places are only accessible by air: and then only in good weather.

During the last three thousand years Nepal's proportions have changed frequently — and considerably. Once or twice during this period, Nepal itself consisted only of Kathmandu and neighbouring principalities yet at other times it extended even beyond its present boundaries. Prior to the birth of the Buddha, however, its history is shadowy although it is assumed that it too experienced the early evolutions of the Stone and Copper ages. No doubt researchers one day will weave their own tapestry from the tiny threads of recorded fact presently interwoven with the colourful strands of legend and fiction.

For much of the 2,000 years since the Indian Emperor Ashoka raised a stone obelisk to mark the Lord Buddha's birthplace at Lumbini, on Nepal's south-western plains, Nepal's tiny principalities remained either locked in their mountain fastnesses, remote and unreachable, or at war with each other.

Left: A worshipper circles the giant Bodhnath stupa ritually turning each prayer wheel as she walks, seeking blessings and benedictions for the future. Prayer wheels are part of Buddhist ritual, each bearing the sacred inscription, Om mani padme hum — *'Hail to the jewel in the lotus'.*

The first recorded rulers of the Kathmandu Valley were migrants from the east of the country, the Kirats, one of whose rulers is mentioned in the Mahabharata.

Some centuries later, between the 4th and the 8th century AD, the Lichhavis, a dynasty from nothern India, held power. Save for a stone temple inscription at Changu Narayan, little, if anything at all, remains of their influence or their era.

By the 17th century, what is now western Nepal was composed alone of more than 44 principalities or kingdoms. And there were three independent sovereign kingdoms — all of the Malla dynasty which ruled from the 8th century — in the Kathmandu valley which bequeathed a legacy of superb temples, works of art and statues. Each minted its own coins and maintained its own armies.

But these only drew covetous and acquistive glances from one of the largest and most powerful of the western Nepal fiefdoms, that of King Prithvi Narayan Shah, one of the scions of the dynasty which ruled the Gorkha kingdom.

In 1768 his armies marched into the Valley and clashed in battle with those of the Malla kings which were unequal to the task — a weakness that paved the way for the unification of much of Nepal and the founding of the Royal dynasty which still rules.

Establishing the seat of his government in Kathmandu, King Prithvi began a campaign that lasted half a century, long after his death in January 1775, and continuously extended the boundaries of his tiny kingdom — until finally, in 1816, the royal armies ran into another royal army considerably stronger in numbers and weaponry, that of the British monarchy. But forty years later, as reward for its support during the Indian Mutiny, Britain restored part of the territory which it had taken and Nepal assumed the proportions which it boasts to this day.

King Prithvi closed his borders to the rest of the world except Tibet saying of western Imperialism: 'First the Bible, then the trading stations, then the cannon.'

Opposite: Patan's 16th century terracotta Mahabauddha Temple. Built by the scholar, Abhayraj and his descendants, it was damaged in many places by the great earthquake of 1934 and painstakingly rebuilt to the original design and specification. Every brick carries an image of Buddha.

Above: Eighth century Licchavi carving of Vishnu at Changu Narayan, a hilltop shrine near Kathmandu.

King Prithvi's able general was Bir — Amar 'The Immortal' — Singh who learnt the arts of statesmanship and war from the monarch. After the King died, he became the chief strategist of the monarchy, determined to see the Royal standard fly throughout the length and breadth of the Himalayan region. He and his contemporaries performed wondrous well. By 1810 Nepal extended from the western borders of Kashmir to the eastern borders of Sikkim. And by his bravery, particularly in the epic battles against the British — even though he had advised against going to war against the British — Amar 'the Immortal' became known as 'The Living Lion'.

All this territory, of course, was forfeit in the wake of Nepal's defeat by the British at the end of the two year war which broke out in 1814. Under the 1816 'Treaty of Friendship' Sikkim became a British protectorate; most of the richly fertile Terai was taken away; and the new western border removed Nepal from not only Kashmir but a good deal of territory in between. And by the time the British returned part of the land, some 40 years or more later, the Royal family were rulers in name only anyway.

Real power was vested in the hands of the country's premier, General Jung Bahadur, after he and his supporters had organised the infamous Kot massacre in 1846 which resulted in the deaths of almost all his opponents and gave him an unshakeable grip over the country's affairs, marking the founding of the *Rana* dynasty which for the next century, in fact, exercised all real power in the country while giving token acknowledgement to the Royal family as titular heads of state.

One device which the *Ranas* used to consolidate their power structure was to maintain Nepal's closed-door society. The country's borders had remained virtually sealed — and visitors rarely allowed to enter — since the treaty signed 30 years before. The British resident and his heirs were the only aliens within Nepal's boundaries for more than a century.

Thus, for close on a hundred years or more, Nepal slumbered, forgetful of the rest of the world which, however, was not forgetful of it.

Soon after he took charge, General Jung Bahadur promoted himself to Maharajah with greater powers than those of the nominal sovereign. At the same time, he made his own line of succession hereditary, too — his office passing first to his brothers and then, later, to their sons.

It was a ruthless oligarchy. All power was bent to the sole benefit of the first incumbent and his successors. Those who stood against them were put down ruthlessly. So great was their megalomania that the *Ranas* went down in history as the builders of the world's largest private palace, now the Capitol Hill of Kathmandu, headquarters of the Government bureaucracy despite the destruction of a large section by fire some years ago. By contrast, the Royal family were virtual hostages within their own much smaller palace.

The opulent, extravagant life style of the *Ranas* was in sharp contrast to the squalor of life outside. Save for the abolition of slavery, they held back virtually all progress — and sustained a way of life that even today presents the living feel of the Middle Ages to all who visit it.

And there are many who do these days, with the numbers growing by the moment. For by thus perpetuating Nepal's remarkably varied cultures in the limbo of things forgotten, the *Ranas* unwittingly created a vast and mainly unsatisfied curiosity about Nepal which has served as the base of a sizeable and rapidly expanding tourist industry — an unintended and beneficial legacy to those, both monarchy and subjects, who until 1950 were the oligarchy's victims.

Indeed, when the revolution did come — from within the Palace not outside — interest in this forbidden kingdom was at its height. Like Tibet, its equally inaccessible neighbour to the north, so little was known about Nepal that it was more shadow than substance, more legend than fact.

Perhaps the *Ranas* had hoped that they could perpetuate their puppet kingdom indefinitely, keeping millions of Nepalese hostage to illiteracy, disease and hunger. But much changed in the century after General Jung Bahadur became its despotic ruler.

At the time he took charge, Nepal was ruled by Rajendra Vikran Shah, a weakling king, easily given to intrigue, and a powerful Prime Minister, Mathbar Singh Thapa, a veteran of Nepal politics who had been called back into favour from exile in 1843 and wielded immense influence.

Indeed, he himself had ambitions to become a dictator until the night — in May 1845 — when he was lured to the Palace by a false message saying the Queen was sick and on her death-bed. As soon as he stepped into the Queen's chamber he was assassinated by Jung Bahadur who had become a court favourite.

The British saw little reason to interfere with the new status quo. They already had their hands full in India and, besides, Jung Bahadur professed friendship to the British crown. Nepal, too, supplied the British army with Gurkha soldiers whose legendary bravery was known wherever men met and fought.

This land, for more than a century in the limbo of suspended time and motion, was in for a brisk awakening.

In the years immediately following the Second World War India freed itself of British dominion, in the process swallowing 500 autonomous principalities and China the giant awoke, shuddering out of its long hibernation, the convulsions sending waves of Tibetan refugees flooding into the land of the *Ranas*.

As mankind began to plan his first ventures into space, this anachronistic and cruel oligarchy was an ironic affront to the new spirits abroad in the neighbouring lands — and well the despots knew it.

The new liberalism influenced the ruling *Rana* prime minister whose response was to propose a new constitution which would grant a measure of democracy to the peasant classes. It would have involved councils of village elders — *panchas* ruling at local level with the leaders of each village council elected to a national *panchayat* — a multi-representative popularly elected nonparty political government. Ultimately this is the system which Nepal adopted but in the 1950s the 'liberal' *Rana* leader was out of step and swiftly replaced.

His place was taken by a reactionary who favoured increased isolationism and authoritarianism — an untenable stance in a world where people were fired everywhere by the ideals of nationalism and independence under a popular elected franchise. The idea was that King Tribhuvan, powerless in his palace, would continue to acquiesce at this mockery of not only democracy but also royal autocracy.

Above: Brightly-hued representation of Biswarupa in his many forms, with the demoniac visage of Bhairav as its focal point, above the Golden Door of the Hanuman Dhoka Durbar.

The Royal family's freedom of movement was curtailed — but not sufficiently to stop the King and his family planning a shooting picnic in one of the Royal game reserves. They used the occasion to enter the Indian embassy in the capital and under cover of their asylum travel to India. They left behind King Tribhuvan's grandson, Gyanendra, aged four.

At the same time that King Tribhuvan was being hailed in Delhi as reigning ruler, the *Ranas* crowned the little child and proclaimed him King of Nepal!

Three months later, after Nepalese freedom fighters had overthrown the oligarchy, King Tribhuvan returned to a hero's welcome and on 18 February 1951 proclaimed the end of *Rana* autocracy. Not long after this, the last of the *Rana* premiers stepped down and went into exile in India. Nepal had emerged from its dark ages to take its place among the modern nations of the world.

Much needed to be done. There was not even a postal service in this land which takes its name from a Saint called Ne and the Sanskrit word for preservation, *pala*.

In a land where four calendars are still in use, the first currency notes were issued in 1945, and a nationwide postal service only began in 1959 — three years after Nepal joined the International Postal Union. It became a member of the United Nations in 1955.

In 1959 — the year the Soviet Union launched the first space satellite, Sputnik — the first general elections in the country's history were held, resulting in a very clear cut majority for B.P. Koirala's party. King Tribhuvan's promise of truly democratic elections had still not materialised when he died in Zurich at the age of 48 in 1955 and it was his son and heir, King Mahendra, who published the constitution which provided Nepal with a Parliamentary government.

Charismatic, strong on mass support, Koirala had led the fight against the *Ranas* and was an obvious choice as Prime Minister but his strong conviction about the form Nepalese government should take were not to King Mahendra's liking. In many ways they once again relegated the Royal Family to the role of symbolic head of state. Almost inevitably, given the century which had passed, within a year the monarch ordered the arrest of the Cabinet and dissolved the Government.

King Mahendra presented his people with a new constitution which promised a system of indirect government — similar in fact to the *panchayat* system which had been proposed 12 years before by the liberal *Rana* premier. Under this constitution, the choice of Cabinet and Premier lay solely at the King's discretion. Political parties were outlawed and the freedom of speech curtailed.

When King Mahendra died ten years later — in January 1972 — the new constitution was firmly, if unhappily, entrenched and his successor, the present monarch, King Birendra, was loath to change it. Though King in every aspect, his coronation in fact was delayed by three years. Until February 1975 the court astrologers did not feel there were sufficent augurs of good fortune strong enough to justify his formal investiture.

Educated at Eton and Harvard, the youthful King matured quickly. Only four years after his coronation, the patience of his happy-go-lucky uncomplaining citizens finally broke when for the first time in the country's history — on 23 May 1979 — rioting broke out in Kathmandu. Next morning, in a nationwide broadcast, King Birendra promised his people a national referendum to decide which system of government they wanted.

It was followed by a Royal decree which granted considerable freedom of speech and assembly. The crisis was averted. Koirala, who had been in self-exile or jail for the last 19 years, returned to Nepal free to campaign for the system of government — multi-party political — which he wanted to introduce.

But when the votes were cast in the May 1980 referendum more than

Above: Eternal snows of 23,460 foot high Ganesh II dominate the upper reaches of Langtang Valley.

Right: Undefiled by man, pyramid peak of sacred Machhapuchhare rises serenely above the fertile valleys close to Pokhara to a height of 22,942 feet.

half the people voted for the existing system — although the King had already ruled that whichever side won any future national legislature would be elected by the people which, in turn, would elect the prime minister. The first General Elections followed one year later, in May 1981, but King Birendra still retained the right to nominate 20 per cent of the legislative members and his Royal decree remained the supreme Constitutional authority.

These domestic affairs were of small concern to the rest of the world. What mattered was that with the restoration of the Royal prerogative in 1951 Nepal's borders were at last open to visitors, particularly the many climbers who wished to tackle its challenging peaks, the greatest mountains in the world. As the 1950s dawned, after more than a century of isolation, these peaks were shrouded as much in myth as in the raging mists, driven by the jet streams, which frequently plume out from their lofty summits like the royal standards of their divine residents.

Notable among the first explorer-climbers were H.W. Tilman and Eric Shipton who opened much of central Nepal and the Everest region for those who were to follow. Two of their contemporaries were the Frenchmen Maurice Herzog and Louis Lachenal who also surmounted innumerable problems in dealing with the inflexible bureacracy left behind by the *Ranas* to become the first men to stand above a height of 26,250 feet — the magic 8,000 metres mark — when they reached the 26,545 foot high summit of Annapurna, the world's tenth highest mountain, on 3 March 1950.

The two, looking down the precipitous south face, judged it unclimbable yet only 20 years later, Don Whillans and Dougal Halston, two British climbers in an expedition led by Chris Bonnington, succeeded in achieving the 'impossible'. All paled, of course, against the achievement of Edmund Hilary of New Zealand and Sherpa Norgay Tenzing of Nepal who reached the apex of the world — the top of Mount Everest — on 29 May 1953.

Sir George Everest, the man who ordered the first survey of the highest point on earth, died in 1866 aged 76. He joined the East India company as an apprentice when he was 16 and went on to become Surveyor-General of the country in 1827.

Since, as recently as 1969, the mountain which was named after him was being listed in encyclopaedias as a mere 29,002 feet high — some 26 feet shorter than its official height in 1986 — cynics may be forgiven for wondering how accurate was Sir George's 19th century theodolite!

An 18th century German map was the first to mark the mountain using, in 1717, the Tibetan name Chang-mo-Langma, meaning 'Mother Goddess of the Universe'. The first theodolite reading was made in 1849.

Nepal's eight highest mountains — all above 26,250 feet — were all climbed between 1950 and 1960. As well as Everest and Annapurna, these include the world's third highest mountain, Kanchenjunga at 28,208 feet; Lhotse, a sister to Everest, 27,890 feet; Makalu 27,807 feet; Dhaulagiri 26,795 feet; Manaslu 26,760 feet; and Cho Oyu 26,750 feet. Gosainthan which is 26,398 feet high lies a few kilometres inside Tibet.

Besides these monoliths, Nepal boasts almost 150 peaks above 19,700 feet — the 6,000 metres mark — of which 49 are above 23,000 feet, the 7,000 metres mark.

In recent years, the pattern of Himalayan mountaineering has shifted its emphasis. At first, during the 1950s, climbers chose to scale these unpredictable peaks by the 'easiest' route during the most favourable weather. Now they are attacked by ever more difficult routes and tougher and more perilous techniques in more dangerous seasons.

World champion at this most lethal of sports is the Italian ace Reinhold Messner who has climbed more of the world's — and Nepal's — great mountains solo than anybody else.

Only fourteen mountains in the world rise above the magic mark of 26,250 feet — 8,000 metres. And since his first successful 1970 conquest of Pakistan's killer mountain 26,660 foot high Nanga Parbat, the schoolteacher turned mountaineer has been tackling them one by one to become the first man to make an ascent of both Everest and 28,250 foot high K2, the world's second highest mountain which is in Pakistan, without oxygen and alone.

In 1980 it took him only four days to climb from the base camp to the summit of Everest and back — without benefit of fixed camps, companions or oxygen. Three years later he had conquered five more of

Above: Dry bed of the Mahesh Kola in background with families planting the flooded rice paddies alongside Prithvi Highway south of Kathmandu.

Opposite: Farm womenfolk plant rice in fertile paddies alongside the Prithvi Highway from Kathmandu to Mugling.

Overleaf: Crew roar a battle cry as they steer their dinghy into the raging waters of the Grade IV 'Up Set' Rapids on the Trisuli River. In foreground water rages in a 12 metre deep hole. Should an unfortunate crew member be tossed overboard, the powerful eddies can keep him trapped in a constant orbit until he drowns.

these giants — in Tibet, Pakistan and Nepal — to bring his tally to a total of nine, including two ascents of K2 and Everest.

By 1986 he had completed his ambition to climb all the 8,000 metre high mountains — reaching the summit of 27,807 foot high Makalu on Friday 26 September 1986 and then marching on to conquer Everest's sister peak, 27,925 foot high Lhotse in October 1986.

Messner is driven by the same spirits that inspired and, ultimately, claimed the life of British climber Joe Tasker who fell to his death from the north-east ridge of Everest in May 1982. In his book, *Everest, the Cruel Way* which appeared the year before, Tasker wrote:

'We never achieve mastery of the mountains; the mountains are never conquered; they will always remain and sometimes they will take away our friends if not ourselves.'

The Himalaya takes its name from two Sanskrit words — the language on which Nepali is based — meaning snow, *him*, and abode, *alaya*. Young by mountain standards, this massive spinal cord of the world was formed about 50 million years ago when India and Central Asia began to jostle each other.

The sea which lay between them receded and as they rubbed shoulders the soft sea bed — a mixture of sands and mud dumped into it by rivers from both land masses — rose up into a series of gigantic folds. Thus was Sagarmatha, 'Goddess of the Universe' created, now hardened into steely granite by the weathering of the ages but still rising, inch by inch, as the relentless forces beneath the continental plates exert their tremendous pressure.

In the years since Nepal reopened its borders in 1950, mountaineering has been the linchpin of what has become its major industry, tourism. Yet it is not these 8,000 metre giants which inspire the most reverence, either among the Nepalese or visiting tourists. Though a diminutive in terms of altitude — only 22,942 feet high — most people's lasting impression of Nepal arises from the symmetrical beauty of sacred Machhapuchhare, lying to the west of the Annapurna massif, with its twin 'fish-tail' peaks reflecting their awesome beauty in the still waters of Lake Phewa in the Pokhara Valley.

Early in the 1950s a British expedition came to within 500 feet of its summit but could climb no further. After their descent, one of the expedition told the Nepalese that at least one mountain should remain forever undefiled by man and because of Machhapuchhare's divine beauty nominated it as the one most worthy of such status. Since then, no foot has desecrated the mountain's jagged slopes — symbol of all that these mighty mountains stand for in both the human mind and heart.

This spiritualism reflects itself, too, in the divine temples which cover the land from end to end. Like a string of architectural pearls, they garnish valleys and towns with an ineradicable beauty, indestructible either in monsoon storm or the raging earthquakes which suddenly wrack the land when one of the ancient mountains stirs and trembles in its long slumber.

Nepal's biggest treasury lies within the Kathmandu Valley and stems from the Malla Dynasty which inspired a profusion of temples, statues, works of art and architecture.

In the late 1950s and early 1960s this 'Valley of the Gods' swiftly

Above: Holy man, sadhu, *meditates on the hill overlooking the Shiva temple of Pashupatinath at Deopatan, near Kathmandu. The Temple is considered one of the most sacred of all Hindu shrines in India and Nepal.*

Overleaf: Elephant carrying an early-bird tourist raises its trunk in salute to new-born day as sunrise paints the sky a glow of pastel colours over forest in Royal Chitwan National Park.

Above: Hindu holy man, sadhu, at a Kathmandu temple. These spiritual ascetics travel hundreds of mile by foot with few or no possessions, their life devoted to meditation.

became the Mecca of the Hippies. Nepal's gentle and tolerant citizens, who clasped their hands together, bowed their hands in deference and murmured, 'Namaste' — welcome — believe that, invited or uninvited, 'a guest is a god in disguise'.

With hashish and marijuana freely available it drew the new Beat Generation halfway round the world like a magnet. Nepal's first experience of the western world was through a stream of string-haired, pot-smoking dropouts, poets and back-packers with little in their pockets and not too much in their heads except narcotic fantasies — or rugged mountaineers seemingly bent on self-destruction.

Amid Kathmandu's medieval buildings and Middle Ages life style, basking in the balmy climate and the fertility of Hinduism and Mahayana Buddhism and the tolerance of a friendly population, the hippies set up court in a narrow lane in the modern capital which became known the world over as 'Freak Street'. Here, where it was green, the 'locust' people settled to eat the lotus, push the pot and pop the coke — and in the incandescent visions inspired by these drugs saw the mystic and the sublime. There were two *Shangri-las* joined by the same rainbow — the gold was in the beaches of Goa beloved of the Hippies and the 'pot' was at the other end of the rainbow in the Himalaya.

Slowly during the 1970s, they drifted away and 'Freak Street' became just another gaudy but faded stop on the well-planned itinerary of the new generation of tourists, the budget-conscious international travellers who have earned the more derisory soubriquet of Trippies.

Cat Stevens sang a pop song about Kathmandu when it was all 'Freak Streets' but now the psychedelic overland coaches and lorries — with labels like Frankfurt, Khajaraho, Teheran, London and Goa — dubbed *The Chapati Expresses* are no more. Only the legacy of 'Freak Street' remains — in its second-hand book shops, used shoes, paper prints of the gods, and the Tantric erotica.

But it is not the hippy legend which saw the number of visitors to Nepal grow from under 10,000 a year at the start of the 1960s to around 200,000 a year by the middle of the 1980s.

They were drawn to this enchanted land by the profusion of its scenery; its rushing rivers, shining lakes, glittering glaciers, snowy mountain crests, and its mosaic of colourful peoples.

With a 1986 population of between 17 to 18 million roughly half a million new citizens, belonging to one of 35 different ethnic groups characterised by their dialect, locale, dress and religion, were being born each year as Nepal approached the end of the 20th century which in its own calendar was the middle of the 21st century.

They enter a society which is a complex blending of two major religions, Hinduism and Buddhism, with a remarkable homogenity. For centuries they have worshipped each other's gods and cherished a mutal respect for one another — from the day more than 2,500 years ago that Gautama, the Buddha, was born.

Such are the delights, contrasts and contradictions that make a *Journey through Nepal* unforgettable.

2. The Tigers and the Terai

If you travel through India you can enter Nepal a dozen different ways. In the east, on the narrow neck of land that connects north-east India with the rest of that vast country — and divides Nepal from Bhutan, another tiny Himalayan kingdom — is West Bengal and Sikkim. From Siliguri in Bengal the road crosses the Mechi River, a tributary of the Ganges, to Kakar Bhitta.

In fair weather there is an alternative hill road from Darjeeling that cuts through the Mane Pass before descending to the rolling tea fields of Ilam, set at around 4,000 feet, which roll away in every direction, a carpet of vivid green laid out at the feet of Nepal's north-eastern mountains.

These peaks, seemingly elusive, suddenly appear around one bend or the other, framed between the leafy magnificence of a rhododendron forest, strands of cloud drifting above the valleys and ridges in between, circling the base of these monolithic masses so that they appear as disembodied phantoms, white on white, floating above the world. But no ghosts, especially mighty Kanchenjunga, have such solid substance as these towering pinnacles of rock.

With its weathered brick houses, gracious Ilam is a gentle community of around 12,000 souls and has a tea factory, where the leaf is cured before being shipped to Kathmandu and the rest of Nepal. Some villagers run cottage industries turning out a range of handmade cloth, blankets, sweaters and carpets.

Focal point of this region, lying at the base of the ever-green Vijaypur Hills, is Dharan Bazaar, both ancient and modern. Summer days, with a haze that promises another fine, warm day, the town wakes early, the market merchants setting up their stalls and laying out their wares while the air is still chill, fingers of smoke from the first fires spiralling slowly into the air.

An unusual feature of town life to the visitor is the flag which flies over one of the squat single-storey buildings. It's the Union Jack — for this is one of two British Army recruiting centres in this independent kingdom. The other is at Pokhara, in central Nepal.

Wiry teenagers down from the hills continue a long and noble tradition enlisting — usually for life — as Gurkha soldiers while those of older generations, now retired, make the long trek each month to pick up their pensions. A tough physical examination limits the numbers who succeed but those that do are fitted out with new uniforms and flown to Hong Kong for 10 months' basic training, thereafter returning home to a heroes' welcome from their relatives and neighbours for their first leave.

After tourism, military service in foreign forces forms the country's second largest single source of foreign exchange — pay, pensions and related services bringing between US$15 to $20 million a year into the country.

The bravery of the Gurkha, who also serve as the elite of the Royal Nepalese Army, is legendary. These short and stocky hillsmen fear nobody. Their noble part in major battles is written large in the annals of military history.

During the last two centuries their feats of valour have earned them endless awards, notably 13 Victoria Crosses, considered the highest award for valour that can be given — most recently, in the short and sudden 1982 Falklands War between Argentina and Britain. The name

Above: Oxen feed on a Tharu farmstead hay rick in the Terai Plains.

Gurkha denotes their status, unsurpassed by any other military elite, as the bravest of the brave.

It derives from the Gorkhali community which raised the first two Gurkha battalions in 1763 to serve the founder of the present Nepalese Royal dynasty. Calling themselves the Sri Nath and the Purano Gorakh these battalions first saw action against the British in 1768, as well as taking part in separate campaigns against Tibet.

By 1814 this force, made up mainly of Thakuri, Magar and Gurung tribesmen, had slashed their way through the central Himalaya with the khukuri — the fearsome, long, curved blade which by the end of the 19th century had become the most celebrated weapon in the arsenal of hand-to-hand combat.

Their derring-do during the two year Anglo-Nepal war of 1814 to 1816 impressed western observers and the British East India Company began recruiting Gurkhas on an informal basis. These casual contracts continued for another 70 years. When the Gurkhas were formally acknowledged, eight units were already in continuous service in India.

Most were made up of Magar and Gurung tribesmen but officers had already begun to draw other recruits from the Rais, Limbu and Sunwar tribes of the east — around Dharan — and from the Khasas in the west. During the 1857 Indian Mutiny they demonstrated not only their tenacity and bravery but the loyalty that would become equally as legendary.

As Bishop Stortford, in a 1930 introduction to Ralph Lilley Turner's Nepali Dictionary, remembered:

'…my thoughts return to you…my comrades…Once more I hear the laughter with which you greeted hardship…I see you in your bivouacs…on forced marches or in the trenches, now shivering with wet and cold, now scorched by a pitiless and burning sun. Uncomplaining you endure hunger and thirst and wounds; and at last your unwavering lines disappear into the smoke and wrath of battle. Bravest of the brave, most generous of the generous, never had country more faithful friends than you.'

In the last half of 19th century these warriors fought all across south Asia from Malaya to Afghanistan — even in Africa, in Somaliland — displaying remarkable endurance as well as courage.

Equally as skilled at mountain climbing as the Sherpas, in 1894 two Gurkhas, Amar Singh Thapa and Karbir Burathoki, climbed 21 major peaks and walked over 39 passes in the European Alps in an epic 86 days during which they covered more than 1,600 kilometres.

Thirteen years later Karbir Burathoki, with Englishman Tom Longstaff, completed the first major ascent of any Himalayan peak, 23,360 foot high Trisul [Between 1921 and 1937 Gurkha porters helped mount five assaults on then unclimbed Everest].

By the end of the 1914-1918 World War more than 300,000 Gurkhas had seen service across Europe, Africa and in the Indian Army. In a battle in a Flanders field in 1915, Kulbir Thapa won the first of their 13 Victoria Crosses, Karna Bahadur Rana winning the second in Palestine in 1918.

Certainly, without these doughty stalwarts, Britain would have been even more hard pressed to defend itself and its colonies in World War Two. Expanded to 45 battalions, Gurkha troops distinguished themselves in action across the Middle East, the Mediterranean and in Burma, Malaya and Indonesia. Two battalions were formed into crack paratroop outfits. By war's end the Gurkhas had accumulated another 10 Victoria Crosses.

In 1947, Britain began to dismantle its empire and the Gurkha regiments were divided — six becoming the Indian Gurkha Rifles, four the British Brigade of Gurkhas.

Subsequently, the Gurkha regiments of the Indian Army did battle in successive conflicts against Pakistan as well as the 1962 war with China. The British sector served with distinction in Malaya, Indonesia, Brunei, and Cyprus and in 1965, in action in Sarawak, Lance Corporal Rambahadur Limbu won the Gurkhas their 13th Victoria Cross for 'heroism in the face of overwhelming odds'.

Today the scions of these brave men sign up for service in far away British outposts — Hong Kong, Singapore, Brunei and Belize, in Central America. It was from there that the Gurkhas were rushed into action

Right: Gurkha soldier of the Royal Nepal Army. The first Gurkha divisions were formed by King Prithvi Narayan in the 18th century. They take their name from the King's ancestral home at Gorkha, near Pokhara, in the Nepal Midlands. Their bravery and loyalty in battle against the British early in the 19th century so impressed the English officers that before long they were recruited to serve the British East India Company. More than 150 years later, these fearless soldiers still serve in the British Army. No single group can claim so many medals for valour, including 13 Victoria Crosses, considered the most distinguished of all awards for bravery.

when war broke out in 1982 between Argentina and Britain — and wrote yet another legend in their astonishing catalogue of bravery.

Described by the Argentinian press as a cross between dwarfs and mountain goats, they presented such a ferocious mien as they advanced on the Argentinian positions that the Latin-Americans dropped their weapons and turned and fled — not wishing to discover the truth or otherwise of the Gurkhas' legendary skills at disembowelling the enemy with their wicked-looking khukuri blades.

In Dharan the new recruits walk the streets smiling proudly at their success in passing the demanding physical — browsing among the market stalls in the old town where vendors peddle potatoes, oranges, butter and herbs.

The orchards of the Vijaypur Hills are rich and productive and surplus fruit is preserved in a recently established canning factory. Dhankuta, the hill capital, stands on a ridge in the hills above Dharan, pleasantly cool at an elevation of 4,000 feet. Its paved streets, gabled black-and-white houses and dreamy ways are strikingly reminiscent of an Alpine village.

In the early morning, the sharp clear mountain air is effervescent — exhilarating and refreshing, like the charge a reveller gets from a glass of breakfast champagne.

It takes about five hours to make the climb up through the foothills, via Bijaipur, to this ancient Newar town famous for its orange groves and its leafy scenery punctuated by many mountain streams, their crystal clear waters dancing down the hills, their grassy banks lined with pine and oak forests.

Forest birds, including hundreds of pheasants, flit through these forests where trekkers and climbing expeditions halt and collect their breath and poise, readying themselves for assaults on the high altitude peaks around Kanchenjunga and Makalu.

The pleasant climb through the green foothills serves as acclimatisation for the lung-sapping challenges ahead but today a modern road winds its way to Dhankuta, its streets lined with myriad tea houses, the market town itself serving as a commercial, banking and government centre. One modern wonder for townsfolk has been the arrival of electric power. The well-lit main thoroughfare means the town stays awake much later these days.

Though only 40 kilometres separates Dhankuta from Nepal's second largest city, driving down to Biratnagar is like crossing an ocean. Just before the Mahendra Highway — which stretches, across the eastern Terai linking Kakar Bhitta to Amlekhganj — leaps across the wide span of the Kosi Dam, a spur leads south to Biratnagar.

In one of the world's 25 least developed countries, Biratnagar is the Nepalese equivalent of Pittsburgh in America, or Birmingham in Britain — the nation's industrial powerhouse, with sugar, textile and jute mills, match factories, small and medium scale industries, including timber products, knitware, nylon, and rice milling units. Somewhat laconically, the ultimate authority on the Kingdom, *The Complete Guide to Nepal*, notes:

'Biratnagar is a place of attraction for those visitors who are interested in the industrial aspects of Nepal.'

Most would hope there are not too many of them, but certainly it can be no demanding task for any industrial tourist worth their salt to pay the town a visit. Although 312 kilometres from the capital, Biratnagar, with a population of more than 100,000, is just a hop, skip and a jump from the Indian border, linked by road to the Indian border town of Jagbani in the north of Bihar State.

Nonetheless, as an industrial high spot the town is a disappointment for it, too, is surrounded by some of the glories of beautiful Nepal. Just outside its suburbs lie green paddy and jute fields and to the west of the city the waters of wide and lazy rivers — the Tamar River, born on the slopes of Kanchenjunga, which merges with the Arun River, with its source in the snows of Makalu — meander through attractive glades of Kapok trees and groves of Banyan trees.

Soon after, they join the waters of the Sun Kosi and broaden out into a vast expanse of flood plains and marshland, held back behind the massive Kosi Barrage which was built with Indian skill and money and has become one of Nepal's major hydro-electric projects.

Even better, besides controlling the unpredictable volume of the flood

Traditional Nepalese hat, Dacca, so named because the type of cloth used was first woven in the Bangladesh capital.

waters and generating a significant proportion of Nepal's energy needs, the project has provided additional benefits.

The major portion of these newly created wetlands now form the Kosi Tappu Wildlife Reserve, a sanctuary remarkable for its water fowl and bird life — and also home for one of Asia's last remaining herds of wild water buffalo, easily observed here in their natural environment. The herd numbers about 80 to 100 beasts. In the whole of the sub-continent, fewer than 2,000 of these creatures remain.

Indeed the salvation of this species — and other threatened species — may be entirely dependent on Nepal's wildlife conservation programme, despite the massive efforts being made by its neighbour, India. With its well-run game parks and dedicated personnel, Nepal is easier to police in the battle against poachers, though its long border with India has many crossing points, some of them simply trails through the cracked, dry fields of January and February.

About this time temperatures begin to climb toward an unbearable June zenith of 35° Centigrade [close to 100° Farenheit] when the summer monsoons and mountain ice melt come tumbling down from the Himalaya, rushing through the gorges of the heavily deforested hillsides, carrying tons of rich fertile soil, to rage through the flood plains of the Terai — tearing up crops, uprooting huts, ripping away whole chunks of road.

In the months preceding the floods, the Terai is wracked by the torrid wind the Indians call *loo*. So hot is it that few vary their garb from the traditional dhoti. Only those occasionally seen wearing the topi, the traditional Nepali hat, remind the visitor that India, in fact, is a few kilometres south.

Some 120 kilometres westward, beyond the Kosi dam, another southern spur leads to Janakpur, ancient capital, so Hindu legend holds, of Mithila and birthplace of Sita, consort of Rama, one of Vishnu's incarnations, who is the hero of the epic *Ramayana*.

Most of cosmopolitan Janakpur's 40,000 citizens speak Maithili, one of the common vernaculars of northern India, for this is a major place of pilgrimage for Hindus from all over the sub-continent.

A brick-paved ring road encircles this ancient centre of learning demonstrating the civic pride which inspired the building of the city and its many sacred Hindu shrines, tanks and ponds of which Gangasagar and Dhanushsagar are the two most famous.

Non-Hindus may find the reverence accorded these watering places — similar to so many scattered throughout Nepal and India — puzzling. Many look just like ordinary municipal water tanks, ponds or reservoirs. The spiritual significance of such bathing ghats, however, is profound. Apart from coming to immerse themselves in these sacred waters, the pilgrims also flock to pay homage to Rama and Sita at Janaki Temple.

Built by a Queen of Tikamgarh in Madhya Pradesh, northern India, in 1900, it uses the inspirations of 17th century Mughal architecture, embellished with delicately carved marble traceries — filigrees shaped with exquisite beauty — as its inspiration. These are seen at their best on the elaborate cupolas, ceilings and tiles.

Others have since added to the grandeur of this building and also the Vivah Mandap — where, so legend also holds, Rama and Sita were wed.

Above: Heavy load of animal fodder for a young Newar girl on the Prithvi Highway, south-west of Kathmandu.

It came about this way.

One day when the childless King Janak, whose name is synonymous with wisdom and goodness, was sanctifying the rice fields so that they would be fertile and productive, he prayed that fortune would bless him with a child — and looking down saw, lying in a furrow, the baby girl who would grow up to be Sita, embodiment of divine grace and beauty, the personification of the ideal woman.

Her father adored her, says the legend, and when she was 16 he held a great tournament at Dhankuta, about 20 kilometres from the city. There was a supreme test of strength to decide the winner. He that could bend the divine bow of Shiva — given to Janak as a gift — would become her husband.

Suitors flocked to the city when they heard of the challenge, all enamoured of Sita's virtue and beauty, eager to take up the challenge and win the fair maiden's hand. Among these was Rama who, with his brother, Lakshman, was near the city — having just destroyed a horde of demons.

Now Rama took up the challenge to win Sita's love — and not only

Below: Tharu farm workers of the Terai Plains ford the shallow waters of the Rapti River on the borders of Royal Chitwan National Park. Numbering around 750,000 the Tharu community is one of the largest ethnic groups in Nepal speaking a language evolved from a mixture of Nepali, Hindi and Maithali, a local Indian dialect.

Overleaf: Array of umbrellas provides shelter from sun and shower for guards and workers in Royal Chitwan National Park as hungry elephant steeds enjoy fodder lunch break .

curved the bow but drew it with such strength it snapped in two with a sound like an earthquake. Enthralled, Sita placed her wedding garland about Rama's throat.

It was a marriage made in heaven, between the purest of women and the purest of men, and so hundreds of thousands of devotees flock to Janakpur late in the year — when the moon is waxing around late November and early December — to celebrate this anniversary with a week-long festival, *Sita Bibaha Panchami*.

Pilgrims walk for days, travelling hundreds of kilometres, to reach the city. Dust fills the air as the celebrants throng the bazaars, crowding around the stalls loaded with sweetmeats and other specialities made for the occasion. The loudspeakers blare endlessly though not every message is intended for the moment.

Salesmen, politicians and the like, use the presence of such large crowds to promote their own interests — though most tourists may well be forgiven for assuming that the non-stop jibber-jabber in fact is nothing more or less than pious orations in honour of Rama.

Everybody joins the great procession which sets out from Rama's

temple, on the first day, the roar of the crowd carrying for miles across the flat plains. His idol, dressed as a bridegroom, is placed in a gaily-decorated sedan chair riding on the back of an elephant which is equally elegantly bedecked in brocades and silks.

Devotees with decorative umbrellas pace alongside the elephant, whirling their parasols, swaying and chanting, to the throb of drums and tuneless flutes and whistles, elbows jostling ribs as the crowd follows the plodding beast to Sita's temple, *Naulakha Mandir*, not far away. Next day, Sita's idol is carried with great fanfare to the side of Rama in a symbolic re-enactment of their marriage.

Not long after this, Rama was banished to 14 years exile in the forest — with his loyal brother Lakshman by his side. During this time, Ravana's revoltingly ugly sister tried to seduce first Rama and, having failed, then Lakshman who snubbed her simply by cutting off her nose and ears which so annoyed Ravana he raided Ayodhya — and made off with Sita.

Back in his palace, the brutal king lusted after Sita's unimpeachable beauty and tried to have his way with her but she made it clear there was nothing doing and, pining for her beloved, began to waste away.

Hanuman, the loyal monkey, son of the Wind God, able to penetrate every place on earth and in the sky, became a kind of celestial satellite, orbiting the world until he found where Sita was held hostage. Then he flew like the wind to Rama who swiftly quit the forest and with the ever-faithful Lakshman by his side travelled to Lanka where he met Ravana in terrible battle, ending in victory for Rama — and, of course, virtue!

Each spring in Janakpur the crowds celebrate the triumph of good over evil at one of Nepal's most renowned festivals — normally held on the eighth and ninth day of the Nepalese fortnight of Chaitra (around the end of March and the beginning of April).

Known as *Ramavami*, elephants, ox carts and horses lead the thousands of devotees through Janakpur in a milling throng. Other *Ramavami* celebrations are held in Kathmandu and elsewhere for those unable to travel to Janakpur.

The town is also famous as the main stop on one of the world's shortest railways — the 52-kilometre long narrow-gauge Nepal Railways which links Nepal with Jayanagar in India. The line, which actually terminates in Nepal at Ramnagar and is used for freight, is the kind of colourful anachronism which delights the inveterate traveller: a time-serving echo of the old British Raj. Still, both railway buffs and romantics will wish it long life.

Back on the Mahendra Highway the road links up with what was for many years the country's main trans-Asia link — the Tribhuvan Rajpath. In the south this enters Nepal at the border town of Birganj and from Amlekhganj climbs through the Mahabharat Lekh hills to the Kathmandu Valley via the hill viewpoint of Daman.

Birganj, which lies 20 kilometres to the south of the junction, has seen better days. Not so long ago, it was part of the Freak Street trail — hippies and mystics queuing at its twin town Raxaul, on the Indian side, for clearance into Nepal and spending the night in one of Birganj's many cheap lodging houses before taking the high road to the valley. But despite the slump, undistinguished by any historical encumbrances or

Above: Slender-snouted gharial hatched in June 1978 awaits eventual release from a breeding tank in Royal Chitwan National Park. Hunted virtually out of existence, Park authorities and the Frankfurt Zoological Society organised a successful breeding programme to restock Nepal's rivers with this unique species of crocodile. When mature this specimen will be released in the Rapti River. Young have an 80 per cent chance of survival against 16 per cent in the wild for, besides hunting, gharial have many natural enemies.

Right: Delicate Chital deer and fawn in Royal Chitwan National Park. Closely related to a North American species, during winter the antlers of the bucks are covered in velvet which is shed at the start of the rutting season in March.

cultural treasures, Birganj is still a bustling industrial entrepôt with timber works, sugar mill, match factory — and raucous bus depot where itinerants jostle each other in their eagerness to catch the next coach to Kathmandu.

Nepal's one other section of laid rail track, a spur from the Raxaul junction, follows roughly the same alignment as the road to Amlekhganj but no engines disturb it these days. The brief 25-kilometre stretch makes no economic sense.

Those exploring the Terai, however, will opt for the western extension of the Terai road which marks the inner periphery of Parsa Wildlife Reserve and Royal Chitwan National Park, wilderness retreats lovingly recreated out of the once fertile rice and wheat fields that swiftly covered the Rapti Valley around the 1950s after the fall from power of the *Rana* Dynasty at the turn of the fifties. The sal tree is a valuable resource, a form of teak.

Sandwiched between the Someshwar Range of the Siwalik Hills, which extend westwards into India and are clad with thick, indigenous sal forests, and the Mahabharat Lekh, for centuries this had been a royal hunting preserve, famous for the magnificence of its trophies and the abundance of prey for the aristocratic hunting parties. The *Ranas* made it their own preserve upon seizing power in 1846 — immediately issuing a decree that rhino, threatened even in those days, was the exclusive preserve of the Royal House. It was lush hunting ground. Foreign Princes enjoyed it too — including the Prince of Wales who in 1921 hunted tiger in Chitwan.

One *Rana* expedition, unsurpassed for size and unequalled as spectacle, deployed a thousand elephants to walk through the tall elephant grass and the ancient hardwood forests. At the expedition's end, after an equal number of beaters had raised the lurking game, 21 elephants, 31 of the superb Royal Bengal tigers, three leopards, numberless counts of deer, crocodiles, rhinoceros, bears and small game lay dead — and Nepal is still counting the cost.

Opposite: Rhino mother and calf in Royal Chitwan National Park. An endangered species throughout Asia, the great one-horned Asiatic rhinoceros has made a successful recovery in the tall grasslands of Chitwan where it now numbers several hundreds. Indeed, it has bred so well that several have been translocated to reintroduce it in other national parks of Nepal.

Above: Camera-toting tourists ride Maharajah-style through Royal Chitwan National's Park elephant grass for close-ups of grazing Indian rhino.

In the most sensible way it can.

Royal Chitwan was the first of what by the middle of the 1980s was an extensive network of wildlife sanctuaries. But before its inception in 1973 not only Nepal's aristocrats but its peasant farmers too had combined with nature to ravage the Rapti Valley. Protected against encroachment by a virulent malarial mosquito, mankind had little enthusiasm for this wildlife treasury.

The fall of the *Rana* dynasty and Nepal's population explosion of the fifties, together with monumental floods and landslides which sent migrants scurrying down from the hills, combined to push the indigenous Tharu tribespeople across the borders of the sanctuary. Using slash-and-burn techniques they opened up the forests and planted rice and grain — and seemed endowed with natural immunity against the endemic tropical pestilences which abounded amid the dank luxuriance of the humid glades and tall grasslands.

This valley forms the flood plains of the Narayani River — known also as the Sapt Gandaki — which here is joined by the waters of the Rapti and other streams and feeders to become the second largest tributary of the holy Ganges just 200 or so kilometres to the south.

The resilience of the Tharus was increased by the large-scale efforts which took place in the sixties to eradicate malaria. Other ethnic groups joined in carving up the former Royal hunting grounds — and by 1972 Nepal's population of the threatened Asian rhino was down to 120 beasts, barely a viable breeding population. The Royal family were as concerned about the situation as world conservationists and began to plan new strategies for the protection of Nepal's rare and wonderful species. In 1973 King Mahendra approved the establishment of Chitwan as his country's first national park.

Initially, Royal Chitwan National Park covered an area of 932 square kilometres. The grasslands were rehabilitated along with the sal (*Shorea robusta*) forests and slowly the game began to creep back from the uncertain havens it had found outside — and to breed again.

An exemplary model of wildlife management, Royal Chitwan and its denizens have continued to prosper. Subsequent extensions have given it a much larger area, embracing smaller forests of khani, *Acacia catechu*, sissoo, *Dalbergia sisso*, and simal, *Bombax malabaricum* — all valuable indigenous woods. Monsoon fluctuations in the course of the rivers have created new ponds and lakes in a park which now covers an area of 1,200 square kilometres of sub-tropical lowland bounded by the Rapti River in the north, the Reu River and the Churia range in the south, and the Narayani River in the west.

By the middle of the 1980s Royal Chitwan boasted spectacular and readily visible populations of Indian one-horned rhino [more than 400], deer [Sambar, Chital, Hog Deer and Barking Deer] leopards, sloth bears, wild boar, wild buffalo [Gaur], monkeys, marsh mugger crocodiles and the rarer tiger [65] and fish-eating gharial, wild dog, small cats, python, cobra and close to 400 species of birds: truly a wildlife paradise.

The divisions of the seasons are sharply perceived in Nepal — except in the lowlands where it is hot and muggy six months of the year. But a remarkable event early each year, normally around the middle of January, is the invasion of Chitwan sanctuary by thousands of grass-cutters. Many of these were dispossessed of their land when the Park was founded in 1973, given compensation and told to move out.

Now they pay a rupee to come and cut the grass for cattle fodder and as thatch for the distinctive Tharu houses on the plains outside. The fields they once tended have turned wild again and it's impossible to spot the previous lines of demarcation — hedges and dykes which marked one plot from the other. Concern for the habitat is intense. Throughout the park small enclosures, protected by electric fences to keep out the wildlife, contain different kinds of grasses as the agronomists and conservationists search for the ideal pastures for the wild animals of Chitwan.

Up to 60,000 members of the peasant farm community scythe through the lush greenery for two or three weeks. The change is remarkable. Gone are the tall waving stands of grass. Now all is stubble and that too is burnt off to encourage new growth.

It is just after this that you can hope to catch sight of the magnificent Royal Bengal Tiger, most powerful and graceful of all the great cats, as it

Right: Blackbuck in Kathmandu's Royal Gokarna Safari Park.

Right: Blackbuck in Kathmandu's Royal Gokarna Safari Park.

pads lithe but muscular along its well-trod paths, denuded of cover.

The tiger is the emblematic species of the struggle not only to save the country's wildlife, a heritage it shares with India, its giant neighbour to the south, but to ensure that it flourishes, too.

Camped in Chitwan, under a canopy of its ancient trees, no sound of jet nor machine to break the rustling, eloquent silence of the jungle, it's easy to imagine that the years have passed Nepal by — that any moment an army of elephants, their *howdahs* loaded with aristocratic passengers, will round the corner preceded by a great horde of beaters.

But not so. Nepal has been ravaged by the centuries and its forests have shrunk under the axe and plough and shrunk again. Now the monarchy and the government attempt to redress the fragile balance but much depends on how well Nepal can cope with the demands of the tens of thousands clamouring for land on which to subsist.

At stake is one of the world's great faunal treasuries. Between the two nations there are some 500 different species of mammals, 1,200 species of birds, and more than 30,000 species of insects, as well as many fish, amphibians and reptiles.

Nepal's Royal family follows history's footsteps in its concern to preserve this heritage. As early as 1500 BC Hindu sages catalogued the sub-continent's prolific wealth of wildlife, some of it — like the blackbuck — unique to the region. In those days they could count the cheetah.

Below: Largest of all the cats, the tiger is a study in grace and power. Yet its existence is in danger. Once widespread throughout the sub-continent, from the Himalaya to the ocean shore, there are few survivors after years of ruthless hunting to the verge of extermination. Nepal's only viable populations exist within three samctuaries — Royal Chitwan National Park, Royal Suklaphanta Reserve and the Royal Karnali Reserve. Adapted for stalking prey, rather than running them down, the tiger has an elongated body, short neck with a compact head and a relatively small muzzle armed with good canines. Its fore limbs are more muscular, the claws retractible. The species found in Nepal is the Royal Bengal Tiger, the male of which reaches a weight of 440 pounds in Chitwan, a good third heavier and stronger than the female. The largest of all tiger species is the Siberian Tiger which reaches almost 600 pounds in weight. Feared as man-eaters, their preferred diet actually consists of a mixed menu of crabs, fish, molluscs, reptiles, birds and mammals — usually deer, buffalo and cows, but occasionally dogs, hares, rodents and monkeys. They avoid porcupines. After pouncing, they usually kill by biting the throat and opening the jugular.

Indeed these, the swiftest of all nature's runners, became Royal acolytes, trained to hunt down the deer.

No more. This fragile, graceful feline was an early victim of annihilation in both Nepal and India: the last survivor was shot in 1948.

The notion of conservation is inherent in the Hindu philosophy of *ahimsa* — non-violence to any living creature. Indeed, the central tenet of Hinduism is compassion for all living things and has been so for more than four thousand years.

In the 5th century BC, sitting in the garden of his birthplace, Lumbini, west from what is now Chitwan, the Buddha, whose philosophy shares many remarkable likenesses to those of Hinduism, issued an edict to his disciples to 'embrace all living things as a mother cares for her son, her only son...'

Soon after this the Indian Emperor, Ashoka, a great warrior king who embraced Buddhism and disavowed violence, issued a decree, the Fifth

Pillar Proclamation, which may well have been the first conservation law in the world, giving protection to bats, monkeys, rhinoceroses, porcupines, tree squirrels and the forests in which they lived.

These counsels and decrees worked well for thousands of years. Even the *Ranas* ruled a Nepal teeming with wildlife while the British, when they arrived in India, thought it a Garden of Eden.

'…wild pig, porcupine, wild fowl, game fowl, and other animals, dear to the sportsman, are to be met with in incredible numbers.' The *Ranas*, Maharajahs and the Imperialists took aim — and fired.

Nothing, it seemed, and so they thought, could diminish their numbers. In 1953, though sick and palsied, the Maharajah of Surguja boasted to a friend that he had just shot his 1,100th tiger — and went on to shoot another 57 before his death. Not even avenging members of the species could tally up those kind of numbers.

During the 1940s the legendary James Corbett stood by on alert for a man-eater to emerge. In *Man-eaters of Kumaon*, published in 1944, he recalled:

'The tigress…had arrived in Kumaon as a full-fledged man-eater, from Nepal, whence she had been driven out by a body of armed Nepalese after she had killed 200 human beings, and during the four years she has been operating in Kumaon had added 234…' In numbers, at least, the Maharajah of Surguja was a clear winner.

Most visitors enter Chitwan by fording the wide shallow bed of the Rapti River either in their own vehicle or one of the game lodge's four-wheel drive vehicles. In flood, the crossing is made by boat. There are a number of overnight game lodges but the benchmark is Tiger Tops.

On clear winter days this jungle has one of the most dramatic backdrops in the world — the stunning ice slopes of Annapurna, Ganesh Himal and Hianchuli stand out on the horizon in magnificent detail.

The credo at Gaida Wildlife Camp, at the other side of the Park, is to use vehicles as little as possible. Electric power is banned to preserve the ecological balance, but guests wake in the morning to non-ecological tea and biscuits. No doubt, after a night filled with jungle noises — Tarzan and the Apes offstage — this is more than ecologically reassuring for those visitors with a nervous disposition.

The tea is served at first light but Chitwan's bird life reserves its real celebration — a chorus of rejoicing — for the moment when the sun first shows its brow above the horizon and then swiftly climbs into the sky. Their song is a symphony of praise for the gift of another day amid Chitwan's lush abundance.

During the day guests either trek through the 10-foot high elephant grass on foot, keeping a careful — and sometimes nervous — eye alert for the rhino which graze through it, or along the rivers by dugout canoe or, best of all, from the back of one of the lodge's working elephants, the *howdah* swaying in rhythm to its measured footfall — and the horizon clear for miles around for even the grass is not as high as an elephant's eye. Unless, of course, the beast you ride is one of the young newcomers to safari work.

Riding elephant is not simply some sybaritic gimmick but pragmatically proven the best form of transport. The Royal Nepalese Army, to whom the work of policing the Park and enforcing conservation

measures has been entrusted, do most of their patrols on elephant back — and Park workers move about in similar fashion.

It's not uncommon to come across a small work force resting in the shade of a clump of bombax trees around midday, the elephants relentlessly foraging with their trunks, their handlers, *mahouts*, even sleeping on their backs, many with umbrellas raised as protection against the relentless sun.

Trained elephants are an expensive investment. More so as the wild herds of Assam in India, which supply the nucleus of both India and Nepal's working populations, are diminishing rapidly. The going price in the middle of the 1980s was around US$7,000 for a completely trained animal. Most are sold in Bihra, just south of the Nepal border at the great animal fairs, *melas* — Sonepur, Singheswar and Khagaria — of the region.

Different from the wild African elephant, the Asian elephant is comparatively smaller but longer-lived, and more easily domesticated. They need more caring, however, than those in the wild to keep them tractable and maintain their health. An investment of $7,000 — with the

added responsibility of providing for the beast's old age [elephants retire at 50 and can expect to live another 20 years] — is not taken lightly as Gaida Wildlife Camp's elephant menu demonstrates.

Each mature animal is fed 15 kilos of rice, a kilo of molasses and a kilo of salt a day — usually wrapped in grass balls which makes the food easier to digest. Pampered living indeed but these creatures, which plod Chitwan's tiger and rhino trails tirelessly with their seemingly benign wisdom and gentle ways, are worthy of such care. Females are used at Gaida because they are less temperamental than bulls. Feeding time is an occasion for the visitor to join in. Guests also receive instructions on how to make an elephant walk forward — *Ageth!* And reverse, *Pichu!* Or lie down, *Tere!* before riding out in the late afternoon for a drive through game country.

Each beast has its own its own handler and individual gait. For most these game rides are the memories that will last longest.

By afternoon the forests have created a level of cool air which rises up to meet the warming currents of early morning. Black clouds gather as thunder rumbles and the first splash of a tropical downpour raises dust.

Opposite: Erosion scars the arid hill farm terraces of Midlands Nepal.

Overleaf: Carved out of the steep sides of the hills the precipitous Tribhuvan Highway climbs precariously up the western approach to Kathmandu Valley where a monument atop the pass marks those who died during its construction. Sheer-sided in many places, sections are frequently wiped away by landslides caused by torrential rains.

Below the forest canopy, a carpet of rotting trees and vegetation keeps the teak giants alive and healthy, some formed into grotesque statuaries by thick gnarled lianas and parasitical trees which twirl and loop themselves around their imprisoned host, parodies of nature's own forms. One could be a coiled snake, another a hunch-backed sloth bear.

Nature is the calendar — the coming of winter, the dry season, the monsoons. The precise week, month, year, even the century, seem unimportant. All phases of forest life are part of nature's eternal cycle. When life becomes too ancient it dies and falls to the forest floor to begin the cycle anew. The fetid compost which rots at their feet daily sustains and renews life.

The handler astride the elephant's neck, brushes the lianas and the giant ferns aside with his steel-goad, and the seemingly ungainly three-ton steed steps nimble-footed over fallen logs. In the dark shadows of a thicket, a sudden flash of fawn reveals the flight of a startled sambar deer. Giant butterflies flit from leaf to leaf and shadows move; perhaps a tiger, maybe a leopard, or possibly just wishful fancy. But who cares? Today fancy is as potent as reality and for a brief while the guests in the howdah may well be the 'Last of the Maharajahs'.

Out on the plains the great Asiatic one-horn rhinos are moving with steadfast purpose, cropping the grass as a herd of chital, shy, fanciful fawn-like deer, edge nervously away from the shadows of the elephants. With its spotted reddish brown coat and lithe shape, the chital is closely related to the North American deer, *Odocoileus*. Males average around three feet from hoof to shoulder and weigh from 45 to 86 kilos with antlers around one foot long. The antlers of these buck are covered in velvet during the winter which sheds when the rutting season begins in March.

The persecuted rhino, different in looks to its African kin, is known in the Nepalese language as *Gaida* — and though regarded in all the Hindu Vedic texts as sacred was nearly completely wiped out in both India and Nepal. It was once widespread throughout most of the sub-continent but is now confined to isolated remnant herds in forests.

The skin is divided by a series of thick, heavy folds — almost a caricature of the body armour worn by knights of old. Though extremely aggressive and capable of great bursts of speed, the rhino allow the sight-seeing elephants to wander freely among them — and surely there can be no finer way of watching this creature which, in one form or another, has lived on this earth for more than 60 million years.

Walking through one of Chitwan's nature trails, trekkers often come across heaps of rhino dung. These primeval creatures always drop their dung in the same place and mark out their territory through these middens.

Back in the forest, a jungle-fowl — Nepal's feral likeness of the domestic farmyard chicken — suddenly struts across the trail and from a low-lying branch a wild peacock takes off in a Technicolor cascade of feathers. Among the sanctuary's prolific bird species are some so rare that they may only be seen once or twice in a normal lifetime. Gaida Wildlife Camp's trail leaders reel off names with computer-like accuracy though, so far away are they, many guests can hardly make out the indistinct shapes as birds, let alone distinct species.

In the Park's river waters lurk the rare Gangetic species of blind freshwater dolphin. Though it co-habits with the crocodiles and the rare gharial, an alligator-like species of these waters, like them it is under threat: villagers regard its flesh as a delicacy and its oil as powerful medicine for afflictions like rheumatism. The indigenous species of crocodile is the mugger which is found in the Narayani, Kosi, Gandaki and Karnali but is under threat from hunting for skin products.

The gharial, long and slender snouted, is under even more pressure but there is a breeding centre in the National Park which offers hope of survival.

One of Chitwan's rarer creatures is the Sloth Bear, black in colour with an indistinct white V on its chest, a comical looking but aggressive creature that lives off termites, grubs and fruits and snores loudly when sleeping.

Park fees are remarkably cheap for the spectacle and the panorama — in 1986 they were set at 65 rupees a visitor. To protect this priceless reconstituted wilderness, the areas immediately around the perimeter forests have been kept as open grass and marshlands and the former domain of an ancient monarchy is now a national asset.

Today's tiger hunters are tourists armed with cameras seeking a living tiger head on a film they can blow up to a life-size image. Veterans, of course, recall the thrill of the hunt — a privilege still reserved for the Royal prerogative and, occasionally, indulged. And before criticising such occasions it is perhaps worth drawing on the experience of those who have joined the hunt:

'Although there is much in the sport of tiger hunting that renders it inferior as a mere exercise or as an effort of skill…yet there is a stirring of the blood in attacking an animal before whom every other beast of the forest quails, and unarmed man is helpless as the mouse under the paw of the cat — a creature at the same time matchless in beauty of form and colour, and in terrible power of offensive armature — which draws men to its continued pursuit after that of every other animal has ceased to afford sufficient excitement to undergo the toil of hunting in a tropical country.'

Captain James Forsyth, an officer in the Bengal Staff Corps, wrote that more than a century ago. Perhaps even committed conservationists will see no reason to quarrel with his observations clearly drawn from personal experience. Tigers thrive in Chitwan not only from the protective umbrella of the game department but also the humid climate.

This is caused by a predictable set of circumstances and unpredictable onslaughts of rain. Hailstones the size of golf balls suddenly rain down out of what, seconds before, were clear blue skies, so heavy that many birds are stunned and topple from their perches — recovering after a few moments to take off with staggering run and uneven beat of leaden wing and lurch through the sky like a squadron of drunken Icaruses.

Suddenly the air is cool again and the dying rays of the sun burst through the clouds before the swift shutter of nightfall, its rays refracted into scintillating highlights like a sprawl of diamonds.

In the sodden watchtowers 40-feet above the elephant grass darkness folds over the enthralled and enchanted witness — and somewhere down below, unseen, the soft pad of a tiger sends a tingle of fear down the spine.

Above: Tharu farm child on the Terai Plains. These families live in airy houses and avoid working during the ennervating heat of the day.

Above: Laughing farm children on the Terai Plains.

Outside the Park, the twin towns of Bharatpur and Narayanghat are the nearest urban centres to Chitwan. Bharatpur's role in the lowland infrastructure is as an airfield for what the domestic air carrier rashly promises are the daily flights to Kathmandu. Renowned for the reliability of its international schedules, Royal Nepal Airlines has an equal reputation for the erratic timekeeping of its internal flights: understandable in mountain regions where weather suddenly closes in but perplexing to passengers waiting in the balmy and reliable climes of the Terai.

Narayanghat, lying on the banks of one of Nepal's three largest rivers, the Narayani, and known as the 'Gateway to Chitwan', in fact, is also a vital administrative and commercial centre of the Terai and indeed the ethnic capital of the indigenous people of this region, the *Tharus*. Narayan is one of Vishnu's incarnations — embodiment of universal love and knowledge.

Thriving bazaars line the town's populous streets which form the major junction on the Mahendra Highway with a spur climbing up through the hills along the east bank of the Narayani to Mugling, the main junction town between Kathmandu and Pokhara on the Prithvi Highway.

Indeed, Mugling is prominent only for the magnificent suspension bridge which leaps across the gorge 300 feet above the rapids which

churn through the narrow bottleneck where the Trisuli and Marsyangdi rivers join to flow on down to the Narayani. The bridge has given Pokhara and Kathmandu a convenient direct road link.

Bustling Narayanghat is growing fast however and with sizeable industries and flourishing markets is also close to something of a pilgrimage spot. Each year in January tens of thousands flock to the nearby village of Deoghat when a major fair is held and immerse themselves at the confluence of the Kali Gandaki with the combined waters of the Trisuli-Marsyangdi.

Travellers continue their westward journey from Narayanghat over the modern bridge which spans the river, veering south-west along the Narayani's flood plains and over the shallow crest of a spur of the Siwalik Hills to join the Siddartha Highway — a direct India-Pokhara link — at Butwal, on the banks of the River Tinau.

Around 25,000 to 30,000 people live in this bustling market town famous for its market gardens and fruit orchards and also its ancient beginnings on the other side of the river bank, known as Khasauli Bazaar.

Northward of Butwal, a small eastward spur of the Siddhartha Highway doubles back on itself as it climbs, in just a few kilometres, to Tansen — a town of 15,000 souls famed for the erotic carvings of its Narayan Temple.

Ascetics wishing to commune with nature — and there's something mystical about any Nepalese hill, its flanks rising seemingly sheer into the azure sky above, little hamlets dotted among the paddy fields, clinging precariously to their sides — make the trek to Srinagar, a hillcrest which offers sight of a disembodied Annapurna massif floating above a wreath of encircling clouds. Five minutes of this on a clear day and, like the Nepalese, you'll need no more convincing that these mountains are the abode of the gods.

Even in the down market scenic league, minnow though it be, Tansen is justly renowned — for the sheer beauty of its panoramic vistas of the

Right: Shaded from the sweltering heat of the Terai Plains a street barber in Narayanghat shaves patient customer.

foothills around it — as a landscape artist's El Dorado. Craft industries and the traditional Newar houses also make the town itself a worthwhile stopover.

And for those who can never have their fill of temples there's another one, Bhairavnath, which legend says, was carried — lock, stock and timber beams — all the way from the Kathmandu Valley by King Mani Kumarananda Senior: one of history's biggest removal jobs. For anglers, Tansen's leaping streams provide fine sport.

Hugging the Indian border 40 kilometres southward as the Himalayan crow flies, in sharp contrast to Tansen, is the Terai's second largest industrial centre, Bhairawa, which turns out the hard stuff of Nepal's liquor trade from a modern distillery and also refines sugar, rice and oil. There's also another British base, five kilometres outside the town, which signs up more of the stout Gurkha military stock.

But principally it's the final halt before the last 19 kilometre lap of the pilgrimage to Lumbini — sacred to the world's 300 million Buddhists as Mecca to the Muslim and Jersualem to the Christian — birthplace of Siddhartha Gautama Buddha in 540 BC.

He was born in a garden under a grove of cool, leafy trees. The nativity is depicted in a *bas relief* which shows his mother holding a branch of the tree with both hands and the Buddha standing upright on a lotus petal. Two angels are pouring blessings on the infant — a carving only discovered in the 20th century after the garden had lain neglected for centuries.

Buddha's mother, Maya Devi, had been on her way to her mother's home in Devadaha when she went into labour and sought sanctuary in the garden at Lumbini. Well into the year — it was the full moon of Baishak, the first month of the lunar calendar [around April-May] — it was hot and humid and the grove of sal trees were welcome shade. This leafy haven was owned by two communities, the Sakyas and the Kolias, made tranquil by stands of pipal *Ficus relgiosa*, ashok, *Saraca indica*, amalak, *Embia officinalis*, and mango, *Mangifera indica*, trees.

The son of King Suddhodhan, Buddha, a Royal Prince, wanted for nothing as he grew up at his palace home at Taulihawa, about 24 kilometres from Lumbini. In the winter when Buddha played in the garden within the palace walls his eyes often turned northward. He would look up and see the distant Himalayan peaks. The mountains were seminal inspiration for what would become one of the world's major religious forces.

At the time of his birth, Brahminism was the dominant faith in India and there was great poverty and hardship among the people. But Siddhartha Gautama, sheltered by royal privilege and decree from life's realities, knew nothing of this.

He was 29 before he set foot outside the palace when he persuaded his charioteer to drive him around the nearby countryside. He saw old, crippled and dead people and his heart broke — especially after the charioteer's acknowledgement that 'it happens to us all'. He was so overwrought he quit the palace and became a wandering ascetic, roaming the Indian countryside close to death most of the time from self-deprivation.

Finally, he abandoned his wandering way of life and became reclusive, meditating on life until, under a pipal tree at Gaya near Benares, India, he evolved the philosophy which would sustain millions through the next 2,500 years and out of which came his name, 'Enlightened One' — the Buddha.

The way was to reject extremes of pleasure or pain and follow an 'Eightfold Path' based on 'Four Noble Truths'. Mankind suffered, pronounced the Buddha, because of its attachment to people and possessions in a world where nothing is permanent. Desire and suffering could be banished by an attachment to rightfulness.

The individual, he theorised, was simply an illusion created by the chain of cause and effect — *karma* — and trapped in the cycle of incarnation and reincarnation. *Nirvana*, the highest point of pure thought, could only be attained by the extinction of self — and the abolition of *karma*.

For 45 years, the Buddha preached his doctrine before attaining *Nirvana* when he died at the age of 80 but in the centuries which have followed sectarian differences have caused splits — so that in India there is the Mayahana school of Buddhism and in Southeast Asia and Sri

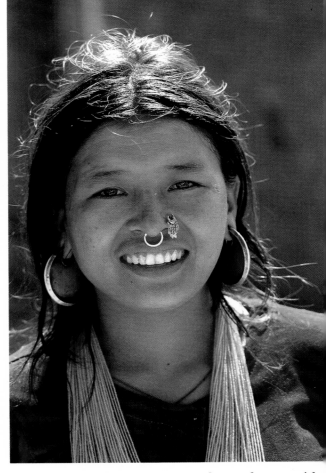

Above: Young Tamang woman enhances beauty with nose jewellery. Living in the eastern and central hills around Khatmandu, the Tamang community — also known as Murmi — is one of the largest of the country's 35 ethnic groups. They provide a nucleus of soldiers for the armed services and farm, hunt and fish.

Above: Old woman of Dhampus, a hill village north-west of Pokhara.

Lanka the Hinayana school, which closely follows the Buddha's original teachings.

Tibetan Buddhism is another unique form of the faith — in which the leading figure, the Dalai Lama, is regarded as the reincarnation of his predecessor. Predominantly, Nepal follows the Mayahana school subtly interwoven with Tibetan influences and shadowed by Tantric practices. Tantra is a Sanskrit word for weaving and Tantrism literally reiterates the Buddhist thought — all things and all actions are part of a living, constantly changing tapestry — but is opposed to meditation. Devotees express themselves in actual experience and direct action.

One Tantric cult, the *shakti*, praises the female counterpart of a god and some Tantric texts suggest that all sin is removed through wine, flesh, fish, women and sexual congress — and some suggest that sex is not only the ultimate form of bliss and tranquility but also wisdom.

No wonder Nepal is known as the abode of the gods!

New ones are constantly discovered or created — one source says there are 33,000 Hindu deities — and at most times the dividing line between the Buddhists, Tantrics, and Hindus is so exceedingly thin as to be indivisible.

Such a land has to be a haven of peace, too, and so it is. At his coronation, on 24 February 1975, King Birendra declared Nepal 'an international zone of peace' — in keeping with the first tenet of the Buddhist religion — and 10 years later it had been endorsed by 75 of the world's nations.

Both the central motif and the heart of this international zone is the Lumbini garden which was not uncovered until the late 19th century when a German archaeologist, Dr Feuhrer discovered a monument — a soaring obelisk — erected to honour the Buddha by Emperor Ashoka in 249 BC when he visited the garden. He inscribed it in Brahmi: 'Buddha Sakyamuni, the blessed one was born here.' Later a stroke of lightning split the pillar in two — a fact recorded by a Chinese devotee, Heun-tsang.

Subsequent excavations revealed a brick temple — said to mark the exact spot where the Buddha was born and known as the Maya Devi shrine — and the sandstone nativity sculpture within the temple as well as other sculptures which have been removed to the National Museum in Kathmandu for safekeeping. Since 1958 the preservation and maintenance of Lumbini has been in the hands of an international committee established at the Fourth World Buddhist Conference and initially funded by a substantial contribution from King Mahendra.

In 1967, the Secretary General of the United Nations, U Thant, made a pilgrimage to Lumbini and 1979 was celebrated as Lumbini Year. Many Buddhist nations have built their own commemorative shrines to the 'Enlightened One' in Lumbini since then.

Tilaurakot — known as the actual capital of King Suddhodhan's land, Kapilvastu — is also being preserved as a heritage site by the Nepalese though the stupas, monasteries and palaces which Chinese travellers stumbled across centuries ago no longer exist. Indeed, very little distinguishes this site from the rest of the Terai in the 20th century.

No greater contrast exists anywhere in Nepal however than that between the Himalaya and the flat, endless plains which form the bread

Above: Old woman of Kathmandu Valley working hand loom in a Bhaktapur street.

basket of Nepal, the fertile soil recharged each year by the floods of the Ganges tributaries which spill out over the wheat fields and the rice paddies and leave behind deposits of rich loam washed down from the hills.

Nowhere wider than 40 kilometres, they cover 24,000 square kilometres and, in parallel with the Himalaya, stretch the length of this fascinating country. Although representing only one-sixth of Nepal's land area, the Terai accounts for more than half the nation's GDP, most of the national industries, provides more than half of the Government's revenue and contains more than half of the population.

This is lush, overgrown landscape, its raised dykes, like those of a tropical Netherlands, serving as barriers and boundary markers as well as roads. Within the dykes lie the rice paddies or great swathes of vivid, emerald-green cornfields.

Thatched brick farmhouses lie in every direction, reminiscent of a Van Gogh pastoral idyll with overtones of Gauguin in the fine-boned dusky beauty of the young girls and women who work the fields.

Already, by 10 on an April morning, the air is hot and sultry and the humidity count easy to calculate by the amount of perspiration you can wring from your shirt or blouse.

Too hot most of the time for any great exertion, farmers and their families tend the fields during the early morning and late afternoon. For the rest of the day they relax, wasting as little energy as possible, in the shade out of the enervating heat.

Such is the contrast between this strip and the rest of Nepal. Indeed, the Terai is really an extension of India in which you would expect a separation of cultures, a difference of peoples from the rest of Nepal. But not so.

The Tharus — the indigenous ethnic group which occupies this corn and rice belt — number close on a million, all mixed up with the many migrants from the midland valleys and the stony mountain highlands who were lured to these fecund lowlands by the certainty of soil and

Overleaf: Panoramic view of sylvan Kathmandu's gilded pagoda temples and the residential houses which adorn the centre of the city, laced with evergreen foliage.

67

climate. And why not? No need to freeze or to scratch a frugal existence when you can eat of abundance and enjoy the warmth of the sun all the years of your life.

The Tharus have been augmented by the entire mosaic of Nepal's upcountry peoples — all living in remarkable harmony yet each reflecting the many diverse living cultures which are still their *modus vivendi*.

The indigenous inhabitants of the Terai — especially those of high-caste — are more conservative and retain rigid values. Two laughing girls suddenly become sombre-eyed and stern-faced when confronted by a camera and run fearfully away over a dyke to hide in a ditch, covering their heads.

The Tharus and other non-caste communities — the Danuwar, Majhi and Darai — live along the Terai's northern edge and in the west. Rajbansis, Satar, Dhimal and Bodo people in the east and Morang in the south. Here, too, in the Terai live the majority of Nepal's minority Muslim community — about 300,000. But the Tharus have lived here longer than most — building resistance to malaria and living in cool, spacious, airy houses with lattice-work brick walls to allow any vestige of breeze to enter. As well as cultivation, they keep livestock, fish and go hunting with bows.

Their bejewelled women are notable for their stern demeanour. They marry early but if the groom cannot afford the dowry he must work for the bride's family — up to five years — to be eligible! They worship tigers, crocodiles and scorpions in a form of Hinduism tinged with animism.

Few tourists yet tread the off-beat trails of western Nepal — despite the presence of the 368 square kilometre Karnali Widllife Reserve, a sanctuary for the endangered swamp deer and, hugging the border with India, the 155 square kilometre Shukla Phanta Wildlife Reserve, last home in Nepal of the endangered blackbuck.

Only about 3,000 swamp deer remain in the whole of the sub-continent and of these, between 500 and 1,000 are estimated to be in the Nepalese reserve making it the single largest surviving nucleus breeding stock of this much hunted species.

Though venerated as sacred in Hindu mythology, the blackbuck has been hunted almost out of existence, made vulnerable by its liking for open spaces. More than tourist attractions, these two sanctuaries are expression of Nepal's concern to revitalise its wildlife stocks and resources. But the new extension of the Mahendra Highway, which now links the east with the west, will inevitably increase the number of tourists to this area.

Capital of the region is Nepalgunj, just a few kilometres from the Indian border. With a population of around 40,000 it has a number of industries but little to commend it to the tourist. However, now that the Mahendra Highway extends beyond it, the future may well see it expanding to accommodate increasing numbers of tourists.

For if anything is certain about Nepal it is that more and more people will be lured to experience its varied and exotic delights — and that the fascinating Terai with its monuments and ancient history serves only as a foretaste of the splendours of man and nature which follow on the *Journey through Nepal*.

In the east, close to the ridge of hills on which Dhankuta stands, lies one of Nepal's most remote and beautiful regions. Nowhere are the country's stunning scenic contrasts more sharply defined or more sharply perceived than in the Arun Valley which lies in the shadows of the Khumb Harkna Himal, below Makalu's daunting 27,807 foot high peak.

Even during the dry season, the wide and lazy Arun River which meanders along the valley floor is one of the few Nepalese rivers that remains in spate.

It bestows a mantle of verdant green and nourishes the cool leafy trees which provide shade all along this enchanted valley and its many companion valleys, equally as lovely. Above, on all sides, rise the precipitous hills which cut off this hidden wonderland from the outside world.

Its villages are typical of so many in the hills and valleys of midland Nepal. For centuries they've remained unchanged. It's like stepping back into the Middle Ages, complete with green-mired village duck pond.

To some romantics it would be no surprise if a knight in armour, on horseback, came clattering down the cobblestone roads to snatch up a shy and lissom beauty and elope with her — or a bucket of night waste suddenly sluiced down from one of the elaborately carved 'Juliet' balconies of the brick houses; to send urchins, pi-dogs, ducks, geese, goats scurrying and hens afluttering.

These valleys and hills, which form the midlands of Nepal, wind their way, higgledy-piggledy, across the width of the country, so remote and difficult to reach that only the passing generations and changing seasons mark the course of time, moulding otherwise immutable communities into living epochs. To take the brief 40-minute flight from the Terai Plains — or the four-hour drive along the precipitous roads which wind through the gorges of the Mahabharat Lekh range of hills — is to travel through the centuries.

When the Royal Nepal Airlines Twin Otter touches down in the meadow at Tumlingtar, the Arun Valley's main settlement, the visitor discovers a world of superlative landscapes and climates.

Like most things in Nepal, it comes as a shock. The images in the mind are firmly fixed: bleak and cold mountain landscapes. The reality is the opposite.

Though northward, only a short distance away above the tree-clad hills, rise the world's mightiest mountains, permanently ice-clad, at its lowest the Valley could be part of Africa. The red bare earth is dotted with stunted sparse semi-arid savannah grassland. Groves of succulents and stands of banana trees repeat the African image. The heat of the sun's rays, funnelled into the valley by the rising hills, is merciless.

Here are no hamlets only an occasional house on the banks of the broad river.

In the temperate region, as the river begins to narrow, no roads mar a pristine pastoral idyll of lush green meadows where cattle, goats and sheep crop the spring grass, rice and wheat grow with prolific abundance and brick-makers use the sun's rays to bake their product for the thatched Tudor-like cottages of the hamlets which dot the valley and perch on the hillsides.

This remoteness, this sense of time removed from the 20th century

Above: One of many ancient Buddhist chaitaya *found in Kathmandu and the Valley; and in other areas of Nepal.*

nuclear world, has endowed the villagers of these tiny, close-knit communities with natural wisdom and inherent belief in the divine. Those who live in the shadows of great mountains seem to have a greater awareness of mortality and yet display extremes of hardihood and endurance few can equal.

The Kirantis, an ancient mix of Mongoloid and Tibetan stock said to have won the myth-shrouded battle of Mahabharat, are a hardy and stocky people, whose faith is a blend of Animism, Buddhism and Hindu Shaivism. Numbering more than half a million and speaking a language that derives from Tibet they are basically hill farmers but young Kiranti men are among the principal recruits to the Gurkha regiments of India and Britain.

Most men, farmers or military mercenaries, carry the wickedly-hooked Gurkha weapon, the khukuri knife, tucked beneath the folds of their robes. Tradition says that once this is drawn it cannot be put back in its scabbard until it has been blooded. Until recently honour was satisfied by the slaughter of a chicken or duck. Now the Kiranti settle for another compromise. It's cheaper by far simply to nick a finger and spill their

own blood to satisfy this centuries-old belief!

In the north the Valley is bounded by the perennial snow-covered crest of the 13,500-foot high Shipton Pass — beyond which lie the mountain ranges surrounding the three great peaks of Everest, Makalu and Lhotse.

Anglers delight in the Ishwa Valley, its slopes thick with rhododendrons and magnolias, its mountain streams alive with fish. Stunningly beautiful, its walls a tangled jungle of undergrowth, rushing streams and plunging waterfalls, another valley — Barun — forms an amphitheatre with distant 27,807 foot high Makalu at the centre of the stage.

It was in one of the rivers in this area — at a height of almost 17,000 feet — that a wildlife expert discovered what may well be the only high-altitude salamander in the world.

A stiff two to three-day trek over the western ridge takes the fit and the active out of the Arun Valley and down into Rumjatar, set at 4,500 feet in the valley of the Dudh Kosi River. Some kilometres away is Okhaldunga, a pleasant village with an old fortress, which has given its name to this lyrical essay of hill and valley, river and lake, teeming with trout and *mahaseer* a fighting fish, that delights both angler and gourmet.

Above: Lions guard the Shiva Parvati temple in Kathmandu's Durbar Square, built in the last decade of the 18th century by Bahadur Shah, youngest son of King Prithvi.

Right: Smiling images of Shiva and Parvati gaze out from an upper window of the Nava Yogini — or Shiva Parvati Temple — in Kathmandu's Durbar Square built in 1790.

On the forest-clad 10,000 foot high crests of the Neche Dahuda hills which look down on the open grasslands of the valley floors are found many of the species which give Nepal one of the most richly varied collections of avifauna in the world.

Among these is the the Hill Partridge which flourishes in the dank forests between 6,000 and 9,000 feet rooting for food in the carpets of rotting leaves and ferns. Another common member of the same family is the Rufous Red-throated Partridge which lives at heights from between 1,000 and 6,000 feet and favours dense undergrowth. Quails and other ground birds also strut around the meadows and stands of trees. Hosts of others, some vividly-coloured, flit from tree to tree — their dawn chorus in springtime an Hosanna to life reborn.

Okhaldunga lies directly at the foot of Everest but few make the exhausting trek through these foothills to the roof of the world and so Okhaldunga remains unspoilt, free of the press of climbers and trekkers, which throng the more direct and popular approaches to the Goddess of the Universe.

And just as surely, west by north-west from Okhaldunga as the Himalayan crow flies, is one of the loveliest places on earth, the Rolwaling Valley, lying in the shadows between the Everest region of Khumbu Himal and that of Langtang Himal.

Long has this valley, shaped by the flood waters which burst out of a 30-foot wide opening in a sheer rock wall on the east bank of the Bhote Kosi river, high in the mountains some kilometres south of the Tibetan border, fascinated those who visit it.

Above: Vishnu Temple at Changu Narayan atop a hill east of Kathmandu. Built in AD 325 by King Hari Datta Verma its glorious splendours testify to the grandeur of the architecture of the Lichhavi era, the earliest ruling dynasty of Kathmandu Valley.

Right: Statues of the 17th century Malla King, Bhupatindra, and his queen, in a gilded cage at Changu Narayan.

Opposite, top left: Detail of brasswork on the door of the fourth century Vishnu temple at Changu Narayan.

Opposite, top right: Destroyed by fire in 1702, and lovingly rebuilt exactly as it was by 1708, the ancient glories of 4th century Liachhvi craftsmanship, in metal, stone and wood, still survive at Changu Narayan.

Opposite bottom: Intricate workmanship marks the door of the Changu Narayan temple in Kathmandu Valley, a masterpiece of metal work.

This gushing torrent, which has already plummeted thousands of feet, thunders through the narrow ravine which looks as if it has been cleft by some giant axe. Many ascetics and pilgrims believe this is the spot where Shiva thrust his trident into the mountainside to let the waters cascade down to the holy Ganges.

It's also in the upper reaches of the Rolwaling Valley that members of the Sherpa and Tamang communities talk about the *yeti* — that elusive Abominable Snowman which has been seen so often by the Sherpa guides who live in the valley.

Perched at around 6,500 feet, with hotels and shops, the small pleasant village of Charikot, just a few hours drive from Kathmandu, is gateway to this region. But progress through the valley — Rolwaling is a Sherpa word which means, literally, 'The Furrow' — from thereon is solely by foot.

The scenery on the valley floor — so close and yet so far from the snow peaks — is again sub-tropical. Amid the sere, baked earth, and the leafy copses of wood which provide welcome shade, tales of the Abominable Snowman sound fanciful nonsense, taking on reality only later in the wreaths of cloud which circle the mountain giants where, among the groaning ice fields, shadows assume substance.

Three dining chairs stand outside the tea house in the tiny 10-house hamlet of Piguti, its quietness broken only by the scurry of pi-dogs chasing a lone trekker through its one street.

Here too trekkers are few leaving Rolwaling's many splendours — including the magnificent amphitheatre of Gaurisankar — to delight only the rare visitor.

Higher up, one, two and three-storey houses cling to the edge of the precipitous paddy fields, now brown awaiting the monsoons as cotton wool clouds dab the little knolls and grassy shoulders with a chill-like balm to ease the sting of the sun.

The paths which climb up the slopes towards the mountains veer left and then right, across perilous-looking rope or steel-hawsered suspension bridges, many run on a toll basis. Slowly the trail winds its way through the forests to the highest settlement — a small close-knit Sherpa community. The 200 families of Beding live in small but striking stone houses with elegantly painted and carved exteriors.

There's also a monastery. Among the many holy places of the Himalaya, Beding is remembered as the refuge of Guru Padma Sambhava, the mystic Tantric recluse who chose the small cave in the cliff, about 500 feet above the monastery, as his place of meditation 1,200 years ago. Soon after this the trail passes beyond the tree line to the land of the *yeti*…

There's something about these mountain regions that make the far-fetched and fanciful believable. But perhaps too it's part of the national ethos, given the millennia in which the Hindu faith has flourished in these parts — nowhere more so than in the fabled Kathmandu Valley, lodestone of all Nepalese art and culture.

Hinduism, in fact, is an entire way of life. Cushioned against the travail of life's hardships by their philosophy, the seemingly happy-go-lucky outlook of the Nepalese is no matter of chance but a carefully evolved acceptance of destiny.

Above: Famed peacock window in Bhaktapur, carved almost six centuries ago. The outer circle of the feathers represents the Universe, the inner circle the sun, the feathers the sun's life giving rays and the peacock's body all living creatures.

This sustains them so well in most cases that in the midst of dire poverty the poorest people — and there can be none poorer — often display the most incredible cheerfulness.

Hinduism seeks no converts nor does it attempt to impose its tenets on non-Hindus. Live and let live is the Hindu credo — all living creatures are sacred. By the same standard, paradoxical though it may seem, it abhors proselytism — the act of seeking converts to another faith. Evangelism is a criminal offence in Nepal — with stiff jail sentences for both proselytiser and proselyte.

It's not only the folk who live in these still untouched hamlets and villages with their incredibly wrought temples which give cause for fascination and pause for thought: so do the landscapes.

Set at around 4,425 feet above sea level Kathmandu Valley is ringed by gentle, evergreen hills touching about 7,800 feet, slate-blue in the misty haze of spring and summer.

The eternal backdrop is the Himalaya which rise up above the horizon — a vista of such purity that for the artist it represents a daunting

Overleaf: All Kathmandu Valley turns out for the climax of the eight-day Indra Jatra festival which celebrates the monsoon rains and the conquest of the Valley by King Prithvi Narayan on the same day in AD 1768. In the city's Durbar Square crowds of women and children await the procession of the Living Goddess, Kumari. *Roughly every 10 years a new Kumari is chosen and each year during the Indra Jatra she anoints the King's head with the sacred red mark of the Hindus,* tika.

Right: A virgin Living Goddess, Kumari, *gazes from the window of her Bhaktapur home.*

challenge. Perspectives are so foreshortened by these mighty pinnacles that few if any can capture them in pencil or on canvas.

From atop 7,175 foot high Nagarkot, the incredible panorama, taking in the Annapurna massif and Dhaulagiri in the west and the seemingly unprepossessing peak of Everest in the east, unfolds in all its glory.

If this were not enough, down in the Valley and on the crests of the surrounding hills stands what must be the greatest single collection of religious architecture in any one place on earth, from the giant mounds of the Buddhist holy places, *chaitaya* and *stupas,* to the sublimely beautiful pagoda Hindu temples with their multi-tiered rooftops. Many say there are more temples than houses in Kathmandu and you find them everywhere.

Since, in Nepal, the two faiths are virtually indivisible these shrines are sacred to almost all worshippers. Many of the most beautiful date from the Malla dynasty which ruled the Valley and its three ancient cities — Kathmandu, Patan and Bhaktapur — during the 17th century.

In these three cities, each assembly of temples, sculptures, and art is

*Left: Crowds salute the **Kumari**, Kathmandu's Living Goddess, as she parades through the city during the annual Indra Jatra Festival. Reincarnation of the original Living Goddess, made wealthy by the gifts bestowed upon her during her reign, her term of office ceases when she reaches menarche. Despite her tender age, she's a revered oracle.*

Below: Kathmandu's Living Goddess, Kumari, now eight, was chosen at the age of five after a series of esoteric rituals — including the absolute serenity she displayed as she walked through a darkened room full of screaming demoniac masks — confirmed her as a reincarnation of the original Kumari. Until she matures she is honoured by the entire community. Even kings defer to her and seek blessing before State occasions of which the annual Indra Jatra festival, when she parades through the city in a chariot, is one of the most important.

concentrated in a central area or square: living repositories of the Malla dynasty's priceless heritage, the most vibrant age of the Valley.

Though much of this heritage, and that of other eras, was wiped out in the great 'quake of 1934, a staggering amount remains. Students of religion, art or architecture, will need as many months to take in the wonders of Kathmandu as the trekker or climber to approach the many mighty peaks.

Though Kathmandu came late to the western world's 20th century — and its own 21st century — it has adapted gracefully. The Valley floor is a network of broad malls and well-maintained highways, many lined with graceful avenues of trees, built with overseas aid. Non-aligned Nepal is able to call on help from virtually every major nation but its principal benefactors are its neighbours, India and China.

The Chinese who built Kathmandu's 27-kilometre long ring road during the 1970s also provided the quiet, pollution-free fleet of trolley buses which ply the 18 kilometres between Tripureshwar and Bhaktapur and carry passengers for a virtual pittance.

Tribhuvan International Airport, built in the 1960s, marks Nepal's emergence as one of the world's great tourist nations though the homely buildings of the terminal reflect the rural tempo of the people.

Kathmandu city's most visible landmark is Bhimsen Tower, *Dharahara*, a 200 foot high edifice built as a watch station which was damaged in the 1934 'quake, which rumbled through Kathmandu in shock waves of destruction, and later rebuilt. For safety reasons, however, it's now closed to the public thus denying what was a popular and spectacular 360° panoramic view of the city.

Between the Tower and the Singh Durbar, the world's largest private palace built by the *Ranas*, is the Martyrs' Memorial, an impressive modern archway honouring those who gave their lives to overthrow the *Ranas*. There are also four black marble busts of four rebel leaders — Shukra Raj Shastri, Dharma Bhakta, Dasharath Chand and Gangalal — executed, either by hanging or firing squad, in 1940 when Juddha Shumsher was Premier.

Kathmandu's Hyde Park is Tundikhel with its royal pavilion where the nation celebrates state occasions with colourful parades. It's decorated with statues of the six Gurkha VCs of the two world wars and around the park are equestrian statues. The park, says local lore, was the home of a mythical giant, Guru Mapa, and each year, during the Ghode Jatra festival, a buffalo and mounds of rice are laid out to supplicate Guru Mapa, and keep the peace.

Of the 20th century, perhaps the most imposing building is the Narainhiti Royal Palace which was built during the reign of King Rana Bahadur Shah and extended in 1970 to mark the wedding of Crown Prince Birendra who is now the king.

Aside from this Royal Palace, however, latter-day Kathmandu's most impressive architectural work is the Singh Durbar. With the restoration of Royal power in 1951 its one thousand rooms, set in 31 hectares of ground, were put to use as government offices. Sadly, much of it was burnt down in a 1973 fire.

Its most impressive feature however still survives — the mirrored Durbar hall furnished with a throne, statues, portraits of dead rulers and

86

Left: Garlands of flowers warding off evil cover the giant statue of Kala Bhairav in Kathmandu's Durbar Square during important festivals.

a line of stuffed tigers.

Today the Nepal Parliament — the Rastriya Panchayat — meets in the Singh Durbar which is also the headquarters of the national broadcasting system. Radio Nepal has been on the air for some years but television came late. The first transmissions began in May 1986.

But technology's graft on Nepal's ancient tradition is only skin deep.

It's best, therefore, before exploring the newer layers of history, for the curious to discover the ancient but still living repositories of art and faith which in themselves provide a clue to unlocking the secret of understanding both Kathmandu and indeed Nepal.

Aeons ago the Valley was a lake which, perhaps in one of the cataclysmic earthquakes which occasionally shake this region, suddenly drained itself. Legend says it happened when the sage Manjushri used his sword to slash a gorge — now bridged by a Scottish-built suspension bridge — at Chobar about eight kilometres south-west of the modern capital where the Bagmati, one of Kathmandu's major rivers, begins its

Overleaf: Statue of reclining Vishnu reposes in a pond at Buddhanilkantha, at the foot of the Shivapuri Hills north of Kathmandu. Custom forbids the Nepalese Kings to visit the 1500 year old statue, one of the holiest shrines in Kathmandu Valley measuring 4.5 metres (15 feet) long. Worshippers walk down a staircase and perform their rituals from a wooden platform. Each morning a priest or temple acolyte cleans the massive image.

Above: Hindu priest presides over ritual ceremonies uring a Kathmandu festival.

plunge to the Ganges. There's a temple, of course, right by the gorge — *Jal Binayak* — that pays homage to the myth.

Whatever the cause, the waters left behind a loam so rich that Kathmandu farmers can count themselves blessed. Abundant rains and sunshine combine with the loam to ensure that everything grows with profligate ease in the Valley. No land goes fallow.

The ox-plough keeps dominion still over the grain and paddy fields and, among the brown-brick houses scattered across the fields without any perceptible form of planning except in the built-up metropolitan area, most of Kathmandu's 300,000 people seem to have a small patch of ground to till. Indeed, from a distance, this richly fertile basin must look much the same as it did when it was first farmed.

Before then, the only communities lived near the shrines and pilgrimage sites which lay on the slopes of the encircling hills. Those that remain speak of eras long before Kathmandu itself came into existence.

The earliest settlements in the Valley go back well beyond 2,500 years, their beginnings shrouded in ancient myths and legends.

The Buddhist *stupa* — a solid hemispherical mound in white adorned by a spire — symbolises the universe and the four elements, earth, fire, air and water. Thirteen rings on the spire represent the 13 degrees of knowledge, like rungs in a ladder, needed to attain *nirvana* — symbolised by the canopy that surmounts the top of the spire.

Kathmandu Valley is filled with these *stupas* of which the two most visible are Swayambhunath and Bodhnath. In the west Swayambhunath looks down from the top of a 350 foot high hill, the rays of the rising sun setting fire to its burnished copper spire as it floats above the sea of early morning mist which fills the Valley. Buddha's all-seeing eyes, in vivid Technicolor, adorn all four sides of the base of the Spire — keeping constant vigil over *Shangri-la* Kathmandu.

The site has been in existence for more than 2,500 years. Indeed, long before the advent of Buddhism, man worshipped here, perhaps at a projecting stone which now forms the central core of the *stupa*. Hereabouts, it is said, Manjushri discovered the Kathmandu lotus which floated in its ancient lake.

The earliest known work was carried out in the 5th century by King Manadeva — confirmed by an inscription dated AD 460, some 600 years after Emperor Ashoka is reputed to have paid homage at the site.

Destroyed by Bengali troops in the mid-14th century it was rebuilt by the 17th century Malla monarch, King Pratap, who added a long approach stairway, two adjoining temples and fixed a symbolic thunderbolt to the top.

Many believe this sacred ground protects the divine light of Swayambhunath, the Self Existent One who, when the waters drained from the valley, emerged as a flame from a lotus blossom atop this hill. Certainly the *stupa* follows the shape of the lotus petal and certainly in the last three thousand years saints, monks, kings and others have surrounded the initial *stupa* with monasteries, idols, temples, and statues which encircle the entire hilltop.

Today the pilgrim and the curious climb laboriously up King Pratap's 365 flagstone steps. Even if you've no sense of religion or history, you'll find the antics of the monkeys, which inhabit the temples and the shops,

fascinating — they use the handrails of the steps as a slide — and the views over Kathmandu as breathtaking, if not more so, as the stiff climb.

Nepalese legend says these monkeys are descended from the lice in Manjushri's hair which, when they dropped to the ground as he had his hair cut, sprang up as monkeys. And that each strand of his hair which fell also sprang up again — as a tree!

During one of the Valley's many festivals a tide of pilgrims encircles the base of the hill and surges up the stairway to eddy around the *stupa*, chant songs and hurl vermilion powder over each other in a dull mantle of red ochre marking the ecstasy of the moment.

Largest and gayest of these is the full moon celebration of Buddha's birthday in late April or early May. Butter lamps and electric lights blaze all night and the spire, glowing in the moonlight, is visible for miles around. Devotees spend the night fasting, in meditation, waiting for sunrise to unveil the hilltop bedecked with hundreds of fluttering prayer flags.

Overshadowing hundreds of smaller images a massive gilded figure of Buddha is carried in a colourful procession down the many steps to a

Above: Holiest and most famous of all Nepal's Hindu shrines — Pashupatinath — at Deopatan. It's dedicated to Shiva and inside the temple precincts, prohibited to non-Hindus, there is a five-faced Shiva lingam. At left of the temple steps which lead down to the Bagmati River is a recess for cremations where Hindu funeral pyres blaze frequently.

Above: Face of Parvati, Shiva's consort, on a lingam at Pashupatinath representing the perfect union of man and woman.

cloister where religious rites continue throughout the day before the Buddha is returned to its hilltop shrine.

Almost 50 feet high, the *stupa* depicts only Buddha's omniscient eyes: the mound has no ears for Buddha disdains praise of himself. Nor does it have a mouth for silence is golden. Nor is there a nose — only the symbol of the Nepali alphabet representing oneness, for virtue, *dharma*.

Mounted on a brass pedestal before the *stupa* is a thunderbolt, *vajra* — so explosive it could destroy anything — representing the divine strength of Lord Indra, King of the Heavens, contrast to Buddha's all-pervading knowledge. Beneath the pedestal stand the 12 animals which symbolise the Tibetan calendar: rat, bull, tiger, hare, jackal, dragon, horse, sheep, monkey, chicken, serpent and pig.

There's a daily service in the monastery, *gompa*, facing the *stupa* — a rowdy and, to western ears, discordant clanking of instruments, blaring horns, and a melee of saffron-robed worshippers.

The eternal flame, guarded by two masterly bronzes of the Goddesses Ganga and Jamuna, is enshrined in a cage behind the *stupa* where a priest makes regular offerings: symbol of the Lord Buddha's first emergence.

Opposite, on a neighbouring hill, the serene image of Saraswati, goddess of wisdom and learning, gazes on the often frantic throng around Swayambhunath in benign astonishment.

Yet for all its immensity, the *stupa* must take second place to that north-east of the capital, where on Buddha's birthday an image of the Master is mounted on the back of an elephant and paraded around the dome. Dedicated to Bodhnath, the god of wisdom, it's the largest *stupa* in Nepal — an immense mound surrounded by a self-contained Tibetan township and ringed by the inevitable prayer wheels, each given a twirl as devotees circle the shrine clockwise.

Most of the worshippers here are drawn from Tibet. The Bodhnath lama is said to be a reincarnation of the original Dalai Lama for the *stupa's* obscure origins are tenuously linked to Lhasa, ancestral home of the now exiled spiritual leader.

Legend says it was built by the daughter of a swineherd, a woman named Kangma. She asked the King of Nepal for as much land as the hide of a buffalo would cover on which to build the *stupa*.

When the king agreed, Kangma sliced the hide into thin ribbons, joined them into one long ribbon and laid it out to form the square in which the *stupa* stands!

A relic of the Buddha is said to lie within the solid dome which symbolises water and is mounted by 13 steps again symbolising the 13 stages of enlightenment which give the monument — enlightenment, *Bodh*, and God, *nath* — its name.

Saffron and magenta-robed Tibetan monks celebrate their colourful and noisy rituals with worshippers chanting prayer verse, *mantras*, and clapping their hands as travellers, especially those heading for the high Himalaya, seek blessings for their journey.

Ribbons of colourful flags stretch from the gilt-copper pyramid which surmounts the *stupa* as the monks blow their long copper horns and, in the crescendo of the climax, everyone hurls fistfuls of ground wheat into the air. Centrepiece of these festivities is the large portrait of the Dalai Lama held head high and shielded under a large canopy. Many try to touch it, sometimes falling flat on their faces as they stumble and trip over the line of lamas who later, wearing masks, dance for hours in a nearby field.

Tibetan folk dancers often turn up to dance well into the night invigorated by liquor and merriment, sometimes a high stimulated by hashish or marijuana, in equal proportions.

So distinctive is the shrine — with its striking colourful depiction of eyes on each of its four sides — that seen from far away it perhaps was the inspiration for the 19th century monologue, *Mad Carew*:

Above: Wife prays for the loyalty and long life of her husband during the Teej Festival at Pashupatinath, Kathmandu.

There's a one-eyed yellow idol to the north of Kathmandu
   There's a little marble cross below the town
Where a broken-hearted woman tends the grave of Mad Carew
   And the yellow god for ever gazes down

He was known as Mad Carew by the subs at Kathmandu
   He was hotter than they felt inclined to tell
But for all his foolish pranks, he was worshipped in the ranks,
   And the Colonel's daughter smiled on him as well

He had loved her all along with the passion of the strong
   And that she returned his love was plain to all
She was nearly 21 and arrangements had begun
   To celebrate her birthday with a ball

He wrote to ask what present she would like from Mad Carew;
   They met next day as he dismissed the squad
And jestingly she made reply that nothing else would do
   But the green eye of the little yellow god

On the night before the dance, Mad Carew sat in a trance
   And they chaffed him as they puffed on their cigars
But for once he didn't smile, he just sat alone awhile
   Then went out into the night beneath the stars

He returned next day at dawn with his shirt and tunic torn,
   And a gash across his temple, dripping red.
He was patched up right away and he slept throughout the day,
   While the Colonel's daughter watched beside his bed

He awoke at last and asked her to send his tunic through
   She fetched it and he thanked her with a nod.
Then he bade her search the pockets, saying "That's from Mad Carew"
   It was the green eye of the little yellow god

When the ball was at its height on that dark and tropic night,
   She thought of him and hastened to his room
As she crossed the barrack square, she could hear the dreamy air
   Of a waltz tune stealing softly through the gloom

Above: Clad in rich scarlets, reds and golds, women feast and pray during the Teej Festival at Kathmandu's ancient Pashupatinath Temple. In a ritual of purification, fasting, and bathing, the women call on the gods for the continuing love and devotion of their husbands.

His door was open wide, silvery moonbeams streaming through,
    The floor was wet and slippery where she trod
A cold knife lay buried in the heart of Mad Carew —
    It was the vengeance of the little yellow god

There's a one-eyed yellow idol to the north of Kathmandu
    There's a little marble cross below the town,
Where a broken-hearted woman tends the grave of Mad Carew
    And the yellow god for ever gazes down

Not that today's pastel Bodhnath, with its red, white, yellow, green and blue-painted eyes on white background, could anymore be mistaken for such.

With about 5,000 exiles living in the Valley, Kathmandu has assumed a distinctly Tibetan ambience with a number of new monasteries around Bodhnath and one, in the form of a castle, on the wooded slopes by Gorakhnath Cave which guards the footprints of a 14th century sage who

Below: Lights begin to blaze at sundown on New Year's Eve 2043 in Bhaktapur as revellers prepare for the fall of the wooden lingam and straining supporters hustle to win the battle of chariots.

Below: Banners, representing the killer snake, swing from Bhaktapur's wooden lingam before it comes toppling down in a thunderous roar.

lived in the cave as a hermit. Not far from this cave the Tibetans have built another monastery — commemorating Guru Padma Rimpoche Sambhava, a saint who rode down to Kathmandu from Tibet to conquer a horde of demons.

But Tibetans are just one of many colourful communities who have made their home among the original inhabitants of the Kathmandu Valley, the Newars. These hardy folk and their extended families observe a constant round of rituals worshipping the many deities whose blessings, or otherwise, rule their daily lives, a complicated mix of Hinduism, Buddhism and Animism.

The Valley's urban society was shaped by them in the days when rival kingdoms held sway in Bhaktapur and Patan. It's bestowed a priceless legacy of art and religious architecture on this mountain nation — and culture, too.

One fascinating tradition, acted out every few years, is discovering the vestal virgin who is the reincarnation of Kumari, the Mother Goddess, who they worship with offerings of money, food and ornaments. Even the Kings of Nepal pay homage to the Kumari of Basantpur. And according to legend there's every reason for them to do so!

For the last of the Newar kings, one of the Mallas, thought her a fraud and an 'evil eye' and she was banished from the city.

But that night one of his queens was seized by convulsions, declaring that the spirit of the goddess had entered her body too. At once, the virgin was called back to the city and publicly proclaimed as such by the King who worshipped at her feet.

Thereafter he spent most of his time in her company playing games of chance with her until one day, overcome by her beauty, he was filled with desire for her. The Goddess perceived his lust and vanished immediately; returning to him in a dream that night when, warning him that the days of his dynasty were coming to an end, she commanded him to select a girl-child from a caste of Newar gold and silversmiths saying she would dwell in the virgin's body. 'Worship her as the Goddess Kumari for to worship her is to worship me.'

Not long after this, the Gorkha King, Prithvi Shah, founder of the present Shah dynasty, became ruler of Kathmandu and Nepal!

Chosen roughly once every ten years when the reigning Kumari reaches the age of puberty, the new Goddess must be an unblemished virgin between three to five years old.

She needs 32 special qualities — physical and spiritual — said to be the sign of reincarnation, including prominent blue or black eyes, white teeth, small and sensitive tongue, sonorous voice, long and slender arms, soft and delicate hands and straight hair curled towards the right.

All this is to naught however if the child fails the final test — walking over severed animal heads in an underground chamber lit by flickering lanterns while masked demons leap and shriek. The young girl who can undergo an ordeal such as this without flinching must surely be a Goddess!

Once chosen she is installed in the Temple, dressed in elegant brocades and silks, served by women attendants, bedecked in jewels, and crowned with a tiara as the guardian and ruling deity of Nepal.

Worshipped daily by visitors, she gives counsel on legal, social and

Above: Buddhist devotee in Kathmandu Valley.

economic matters in return for which she is showered with gifts and cash. Each move and gesture she makes is considered significant — either as a good or bad omen.

Even King Birendra consults her before the annual eight-day Indra Jatra festival for assurance that all augurs well. She anoints him on the forehead with the Hindu's sacred red mark, the *tika*, and he presses his forehead on her feet.

Then, watched by foreign and Nepalese dignitaries, she is carried from her Temple to a large chariot for her feet must not touch the ground.

Sheep or goats are laid in the path of the juggernaut's wheels, sacrifices to save those who in the thick press of people may stumble or fall before the giant vehicle.

King Birendra and his queen watch from the balcony of the palace opposite the three-story Temple which has beautiful carved windows including a 17th century peacock window of matchless detail.
The festival celebrates the release of Indra, the King of Gods, who disguised as an ordinary mortal was arrested for stealing flowers in Kathmandu. When his mother came down to earth to find him, the people, overcome with remorse, fell down before them and then carried them in triumph through the streets in a week-long festival.

Above: Patan's 16th century Durbar Square. Left, is the white plastered profile of the 16th century Narsingha Temple dedicated to Narasimha, the fourth incarnation of Vishnu; partly hidden by the column is the 16th century Temple built by King Purendra, regarded as the oldest in Patan. Centre of the picture is one of the masterpieces of Nepal architecture, the Krishna temple, built of stone by King Siddhi Narsimha Malla, in 1637. Its greatest beauty is the narrative friezes from the Ramayana Mahabharatra epics carved around it. The statue to the right is a large bronze of Garuda. And on its right stand the Viswanath (1627) and Bhimsen temples. The Bhimser temple was razed by fire in the 17th century and damaged in the 'quake of 1934.

Above: Hooded cobra guards bronze statue of Yoganarendra Patan's Durbar Square. The King ruled from 1684 to 1705.

As soon as she reaches menarche she is no longer divine and returns home, an ordinary but wealthy citizen, free to marry if there's man brave enough. It's said he who takes a Kumari's virginity dies early!

Each stage of life — from birth, through childhood and maturity, to death — is marked with colourful ceremonies by the Newar. In a land where people can expect to live for fewer than 50 years, the old are venerated. When a man reaches the golden age of 77 years, seven months and seven days, there's a re-enactment of the rice-feeding ceremony, *pasni* which marks the seventh month of every male child.

He's hoisted on a caparisoned palanquin and paraded through the town, his wife following behind on a second palanquin. He's given a symbolic gold ear-ring which for the rest of his life marks him out as a wise one.

Death is marked by cremation at any one of the many burning places near the holy Hindu bathing places, *ghats,* which in Kathmandu in particular line the banks of the Bagmati River.

All walk around the body three times before placing a funeral fire on the mouth of the dead. As the priest sets the funeral pyre ablaze, relatives shave their heads and ritually purify themselves with the slimy scum-laden waters of the river after which the ashes are scattered in the Bagmati and the priest carries the soul to the abode of Yama, the god of death, where it will merge with the divine.

Descended from the Mongols, the Newars make every day a celebration of life and death. Once a year they honour one of the family cows, usually a calf, which personifies Lakshmi, the Goddess of Wealth, treating it to grain and fruit. Windows are lit throughout the night to please her divinity as she circles the earth at midnight and bring her blessings on cash boxes and grain stores.

Young Newar girls are symbolically married to Vishnu and thus, 'married for life', escape any stigma if widowed or divorced from their earthly husband.

These little sisters also pay homage to their brothers — often their only source of support in old age — during the Tihar Bhaitika festival when the boys, seated behind decorative symbols of the universe, *Mandals*, receive the mark of the *tika* and the blessing: 'I plant a thorn at the door of death; may my brother be immortal.'

Long ago these folk adopted the Hindu caste system ranking hereditary occupations such as carpentry, sculpture, stonework, goldsmithing and others according to ritual purity. Their crafts and artistry adorn almost every niche of this fascinating Valley and its cities, a lodestone of priceless, creative wealth.

Natural wealth, too, blossoms in this fecund spot so like a second Eden. Nepal's flora enchanted early European visitors who exported it lock, stock and root to their own climes. In the words of Nobel laureate Rudyard Kipling:

> Still the world is wondrous large —
> seven seas from marge to marge —
> And it holds a vast of various kinds of man;
> And the wildest dreams of Kew
> are the facts of Kathmandu

Though sadly deforested during the last half century, Nepal's wonders are still thick on the ground for those prepared to look for them. Perhaps the easiest place to see much of its unique flora is at Godovari Royal Botanical Gardens at the foot of the Valley's highest point, 9,000 foot high Pulchoki Hill, where the sacred waters of the Godovari spring from a natural cave. Every 12 years, thousands of pilgrims journey from all over Nepal and India to bathe in these divine waters.

But Godovari's real majesty is its forests and floral sanctuaries — the orchid and cacti houses, the fern, Japanese, physic and water gardens. Throughout, by lily ponds and on grassy slopes, the visitor finds rest and shade in thatched shelters.

Godovari has some 66 different species of fern, 115 orchids, 77 cacti and succulents, and about 200 trees and shrubs as well as many ornamentals — only a small proportion of the country's 6,500 botanical species!

But even Kathmandu's floral glories pale alongside its art and architecture and it's on another hilltop that its oldest temple, Changu Narayan, stands in almost derelict splendour; its struts and surroundings detailed with hundreds of delicately-carved erotic depictions which for many will be simply too indelicate.

For the worshippers of old the explicit sexual nature of much art and temple decoration, worked out, as here, in astonishing detail was profoundly significant.

Founded around the fourth century AD and described as representative of 'the very best in Nepalese art and architecture' it's hard indeed to imagine a more stunning example of what Kathmandu Valley is all about.

Woodwork, metalwork, and stonework combine in dazzling harmony nowhere to more effect than in the sculptures of Bhupatindra, the 17th century Malla King and his Queen. There's also a man-sized figure of Garuda, with a coiled snake around his neck, close to the country's oldest stone inscription, a record of the military feats of King Mana Deva who ruled from AD 464 to AD 491. And though in the intervening centuries fire and earthquake have damaged Changu Narayan and its environs often, this link with its ancient past still remains, hard by an image of a lion-faced Vishnu ripping the entrails out of his enemy.

Life's rhythms here in the cobblestone square are unchanged too with its pilgrim's platforms and lodges, *dharmsalas*, surrounding it and the central temple. Cows, chickens, pi-dogs and snotty-nosed urchins wander around while women hang their saris out to dry in the warm evening sunlight which, like some pastoral idyll of old, bathes the red brick in glowing orange.

From the high point of the hill Kathmandu's majestic panorama unfolds in a 360° sweep — and down there, at Deopatan, is Pashupatinath, holiest and most famous of all Nepal's Hindu shrines.

Set on the banks of the Bagmati, where it leaves a once-forested gorge, it's reserved exclusively for Hindu worshippers. For a proper perspective, there's a series of terraces on the opposite bank — thickly populated with hundreds of rhesus monkeys, regarded by Hindu believers as kin of the gods, sun and stars — where it's possible to study the classic proportions of the pagoda's gilded copper roof sadly

Above: Sculptures of Hindu and Buddhist gods encircle the ornamental pool where Patan's 17th century Kings and Queens bathed. A large stone snake, known as Nagbandh, coils protectively around the outer circle warding off evil spirits. The carving above the tap in the centre depicts Vishnu and Laksmi. The miniature temple above it is a copy of the Krishna Mandir.

surrounded by tatty, corroded tin roofs and despoiled by higgledy-piggledy power lines.

There was a temple here as early as the first century AD and long before — in the third century BC — what may well have been the Valley's first settlement.

In the age of mythology Lord Shiva and his consort lived here by this tributary of the holy Ganges and it's reckoned a more sacred place of pilgrimage than even Varanasi on the Ganges. The Hindu holy men, *sadhus*, dressed in cinder ash and loin cloth, looking immensely wise and benign — but still wanting cash for picture sessions — sit cross-legged everywhere meditating within, surrounded by the Temple's delicate gold and silver filigree work.

To the visitor, the most astonishing thing about almost any Hindu shrine is its shabbiness. It's best to bear in mind that after centuries of use these are not monuments or museums but living places of worship, in many cases sadly in need of immediate work to preserve their glories. Pashupatinath is no exception. Much of the exterior is close to collapse, stained with the patina of centuries and with litter lying everywhere.

Its most precious treasure is a *lingam,* or phallic symbol, representing the sexual organ of Shiva — the Destroyer in the Hindu trinity which also includes Brahma, the Creator, and Vishnu, the Preserver. The *lingam* is stepped in a representation of the female sex organ, *yoni,* of Parvati — Shiva's consort.

In Nepal, the Shiva cult is the most popular form of Hindu worship, above all in his most gentle manifestation as Pashupati, the shepherd, or literally 'Lord of the Animals'.

This particular *lingam* has five faces, one on each side and an amorphous one on top and is said to be endowed with cosmic power! It's well-guarded for only priests are allowed to enter the precinct where it's kept; perhaps because Pashupati is believed to be an alchemist who can turn base metal into gold.

Shivaists — worshippers of Shiva — regard the *lingam* as the fountain of life and the source of pleasure, according to Nepalese religious authorities. Swami Hariharannanda Saraswati in the 1941 treatise, *Karaparati,* says: 'The symbol of the Supreme Being (*Purusha*), the formless, the changeless, the all-seeing eye, is the symbol of masculinity, the phallus or *lingam.* The symbol of the power that is Nature, the source of all that exists, is the female organ or the *yoni.*' Only under the shape of a *lingam* can Shiva, the giver of seeds, be enveloped within the *yoni* and be manifested.

For Shiva is the giver of enjoyment.

'Pleasure dwells in the sex organ,' writes Saraswati, 'in the cosmic *lingam* and *yoni* whose union is the essence of enjoyment. In the world also, all love, all lust, all desire is a search for enjoyment...Divinity is the object of love because it is pure enjoyment...The whole universe springs forth from enjoyment; pleasure is found at the root of everything. Perfect love itself is the transcendent joy of being.'

Hindus have many phallic symbols — one shaped like an egg, one that is a formless mass, one as an altar fire, one as an arrow, one as a light. The shiva *lingam* is always represented in erect form. Divided into three parts, the lowest part is square and concealed in the pedestal, the second is octagonal and set in the *yoni* and the third is cylindrical and rises above the *yoni.*

Pashupatinath is not far from the forested slopes of Gokarna close to the open glades and myriad birds of a Royal Game Sanctuary that's now a safari park for citizen recreation; and for those who fancy a touch of Maharajah style travel a lone elephant plods across the nine-hole golf course among herds of grazing chital, rare blackbuck and other deer, rabbits, monkeys, and pheasants.

There's also a magnificent Royal Bengal tiger in a well-planned but strongly fenced natural sanctuary. The fence is needed. The tiger is a notorious man-eater which once terrorised villagers on the Terai Plains. Its fearsome roars and its anger when roused by spectators rattling its fence leave no doubt about its loathing — and its taste — for the human race.

Just over the forested crest of Gokarna can be heard the muffled roar of the international jets taking off at Tribhuvan International Airport but even this cannot diminish the peace and solitude of this tranquil park and woodland.

Despite their religious significance no such tranquility can be enjoyed on the teeming sidewalks outside the major temples of Kathmandu and the Valley. In the city itself, the main *piazza* is just off Freak Street, the end of the rainbow for the dropouts and the hippies of the '60s who strummed Beatles and Beach Boys numbers on their guitars just off New Road which leads into the main Durbar Square opposite the Kumari Bahal.

Pause awhile to gather your breath when you enter the square and not from the exertion of getting there. It's a sweep of incredible instant images: shuttered, carved, leaded windows and timbered gables, metal and stone statues of man and beasts and Gods and Goddesses, in every material including gold and silver, and buildings both oriental and baroque and many other styles, all quite unlike anything anywhere else in the world. The only equals this place has are just a few kilometres down the road in Patan and Bhaktapur — and nothing else.

There's scholarly dispute about some of the historical detail of each of

Above: Refreshing coconut slices, spiced with onion rings, carried aloft by a street vendor in ancient Bhaktapur.

these pristine works of art and architecture but that should not concern the visitor.

Immediately as you enter the square there's a Narayan temple with a raised 17th century grey-stone statue of Vishnu's personal vehicle, Garuda, in a kneeling position outside. What's inside nobody's quite sure since the inner sanctum has long been closed.

Facing it is the Gaddi Baithak, an ornate annexe of the old Royal Palace built early in the 20th century by a *Rana* premier, Chandra Shamsher, during the reign of King Tribhuvan Bir Bikram Shah Dev. It's here that Nepal's top brass gather with the Royal Family to celebrate Indra Jatra and other festivals and state occasions. There's a throne for King Birendra in the main room which is lined with portraits of his ancestors.

On the other side of the square, behind the Narayan mandir is a temple dedicated to Kamdeva, God of Love and Lust, built by King Bhupatindra's mother, Riddhi Laxmi, and adorned with an immaculate sculpture of Vishnu with Lakshmi.

Close by, on a flank of Vishnumati Bridge, is the 14th century wooden Kasthamandap built from the wood of a single tree from which it derives

106

Left: Statue of Sardul, the mythical griffin defender of the deities, guards the temple of Rudhra Varna Maha Vihar in Patan.

its Sanskrit name: wood, *Kastha*, and pavilion, *Mandap*. It's also from this structure, renovated in the 17th century, that Kathmandu takes its name. Built in the pagoda-style, with balconies and raised platforms, it was for many years a place for Tantric worship but is now a shrine with an image of Gorakhnath, a deified yoga disciple of Shiva, as its centrepiece.

Opposite this inspiring fountainhead of the capital, on the corner of Chikan Mugal, is the lion house, *Singha Satal* — built from the surplus timber left over from the Kasthamandap — with a second storey balcony and several small shops on the ground floor.

Standing in the shadows of the Laxmi Narayan is a small 19th century

Right: Chillis and grain drying in a Bhaktapur square.

temple, built by King Surendra Bir Bakram Shah Dev and dedicated to Ganesh the elephant-headed God, where the Kings of Nepal worship before their coronation.

Near the temple to the God of Love and Lust is an 18th century temple dedicated to Shiva Parvati, Nava Yogini, guarded by lion statues and opposite this is another dedicated to the Goddess Bhagvati. Move along past the Big Bell and a stone temple dedicated to Vishnu and you'll come to a Krishna Temple.

It's diagonally opposite the entrance of the Durbar Square's inner treasury, the Hanuman Dhoka piazza, which derives its name from a

Left: For centuries, potters have practised their delicate skills in Bhaktapur's famous Pottery Market.

large statue of Hanuman the demi-god and the Nepalese word for gate, *dhoka*.

All this is something of a Royal mall. For three centuries or more, the Kings of Nepal have been enthroned in this precinct. The first most noticeable feature is the house on the corner overlooking the Durbar Square which has three distinctive carved windows on one side where the Malla kings used to watch processions and festivals. Two of them are

Right: Smiling vegetable vendor in Bhaktapur with an array of the Sal tree leaves used as a tray on which to present offerings during festivals.

carved from ivory, a discovery only made in 1975 during preparations for King Birendra's coronation.

Next door you'll find another large, latticed window with a gargoyle of a face — a grinning mask in white of Bhairav — carved in the 18th century by Rana Bahadur Shah to ward off evil. It's still there offering benedictions. Each Indra Jatra festival thousands clamour to siphon off sanctified rice beer, *Jand*, from the back of its mouth as it's poured through the grinning orifice. They'll be particularly blessed, it's believed, even if cursed with a hangover next day.

The old Royal Palace — some parts of it have withstood the ravages of

Above: Toothache totem serves suffering citizens of Khatmandu who punch a nail through a gilded image of the God of Toothache, Vaisha Dev. Symbolically pinning down all evil spirits and influences, the act suppposedly banishes all pain.

six centuries — stands next door and is difficult to miss not only for its scale and form but also because of its massive golden door, guarded by stone lions.

Elaborately decorated with intricate motifs and emblems, it's a fitting entrance for kings-to-be. In the courtyard inside, on 24 February 1975, King Birendra was crowned King of Nepal. At each corner of the palace stands a coloured tower representing one of Kathmandu's four cities — the fourth is Kirtipur.

The Hanuman statue stands at the gate and just by its right hand side a low fence guards an inscribed 17th century dedication to the Goddess Kalika on a plaque set into the wall. The inscription in at least 15 different languages — among them English, French, Persian, Arabic, Hindi, Kashmiri and, of course, Nepali — was written by King Pratap Malla, a gifted linguist and poet. Facing the Hanuman Dhoka there's the 16th century Jagannath Temple, outstanding for the erotic carvings on its struts.

But all these temples are trifles compared to the Taleju Temple which rises from a mound to the right of the Palace, considered the most

Right: Dentist's shop in Kathmandu. When nailing down evil at the toothache totem of Vaisha Dev, God of Toothache, fails, anguished Nepalese consult their friendly, neighbourhood dentist.

beautiful temple in Kathmandu. Dedicated to Taleju Bhavani, the tutelary goddess of the Malla dynasty who was a consort of Shiva, the three-story temple reaches about 120 feet in height and each of the three pagoda roofs is gilded with copper and embellished with hanging bells. Only open to the public once a year, nobody but members of the Royal family are allowed to enter the main sanctum.

For anything its equal you'll have to move on to Bhaktapur or Patan and, unless you want a surfeit of erotica and temples and statues, by the time you've walked around both you'll have enough memories of Kathmandu's man-made treasures to last your lifetime.

It was in Patan that the Malla kings ruled, lived and worshipped. Right at the entrance to its Durbar Square, another Royal mall, is an octagonal Krishna Temple. Nearby there's an immense copper bell which was cast in the 18th century by Vishnu Malla and his Queen, Chandra Lakshmi.

Traditionally, it's deep sonorous clanging summoned worshippers but it was also used as an early warning system in the event of emergencies: fires, 'quakes and raiding armies. How the people of Patan distinguished the difference between the call to divine duty and the need to make a getaway remains unexplained.

Set next to the Krishna Temple is a three-storeyed Vishnu temple notable for its tympanums, the ornate triangular recesses set between the cornices of its low gables.

One of Patan's oldest temples, traditionally believed to have been built around 1566 by King Purendra although lately architectural historians suspect it belongs to the 17th century, is Charanarayan. The struts of this two-storey pagoda building, embellished with lively erotica — either inspiring or inspired by the Kama Sutra — will impress enthusiasts of gymnastics.

The centrally placed Krishna Temple is unmistakeable. One of the most beautiful temples in the country, generally regarded as a masterpiece of Nepalese architecture, it's built entirely of limestone, a legacy of King Siddhi Narsimha Mall who reigned for 41 years in the 17th century. The most attractive feature of this temple, which around

August-September each year attracts thousands of devotees celebrating Krishna's birthday, is the narrative carving on the frieze — depicting the stories of the epic Mahabharata and Ramayana.

It was the king's son, Shri Nivasa Malla, who in 1682 restored the undated Bhimsen Temple after it was damaged by fire. Since then it's been restored once again following the 1934 'quake. The Gods make Kathmandu tremble frequently!

Not only the Gods. When King Prithvi Narayan Shah swept into the Valley in 1768 to oust the Mallas, Patan's 14th century Royal Palace was badly damaged but its ornate gates, delicately-carved struts, statues and open courtyards, and many of its rooms — conference halls, sleeping chambers, kitchens and so forth — remain to recall the glory of the era of Malla architectural splendour.

One of those many splendours was the 18th century Taleju Temple which was actually built as an additional storey to the Palace itself and tragically destroyed in 1934. Now rebuilt, it's open for only 10 days each year, during the September-October Dashain festival. It's smaller temple — Taleju Bhavani — though not as impressive is held more sacred.

Of its statuary, Patan's most imposing monument is the sculpture of King Yoganarendra Malla seated on a lotus which stands atop a 20 foot high pillar in front of the Degatule Taleju Temple.

He ruled at the beginning of the 17th century and is the subject of a still popular belief among Patan folk that one day he will return to take up his rule again. For this reason, one door and one window in the Palace always remain open to welcome him.

Patan's treasures are not confined to the immediate precincts of its Durbar Square. Five minutes walk away there's a Golden Buddhist temple and another Buddha shrine, Mahabuddha, two kilometres distant. There's also Kumbheshwar, one of the two five-storeyed temples in Kathmandu Valley. Here Shiva is believed to stay for six months every year during the winter before leaving to spend his summer with Parvati on the crest of Gaurisankar.

About 16 kilometres out of Kathmandu is Bhaktapur, eastern gateway of the Valley, founded in the mists of time but in its present form dating back to the 9th century when King Anand Malla made it his seat in AD 889.

Mainly a Hindu town, its Durbar Square is probably the most visited of the three historic cities, nicely compacted and only a brief walk from the tallest and most popular of Nepal's pagoda temples, Nyatapola.

It's usually overrun with tourists who sometimes stand in the square stunned not only by the incredible dimensions of the temple but also by the non-stop hurly-burly of hawkers, pedestrians and children which occupy the place day and seemingly night.

Most seek sanctuary in the tea room which stands opposite where a good hour can be spent sipping the piquant local tea and studying the erotica on the tea room struts. Built in similar style to the temple but more recently, the tea room building has been restored and preserved, and perhaps fittingly so, by West Germany's concern for their historic nature.

Nyatapola is the other of the Valley's five-storeyed temple. From as far back as you can stand it looks like a fretted pyramid climbing up to the

Left: Street dice game draws gamblers in Kathmandu.

clouds, reaching a height of more than 100 feet. Its inspiration is said to have been as a form of appeasement to the terrifying menace of Bhairav who stands in another temple. There seems to be more than just fancy to this tale. Now more than 200 years old its doors were sealed and bolted when the builders finished their job and have never been opened since.

What's inside is anybody's guess. Certainly, no menace terrifies the hordes who swarm over its plinth and up its steps which are guarded on each side by legendary sentinels — Jaya Mal and Patta, two wrestlers said to have the strength of 10 men at the bottom; next two huge elephants, each 10 times stronger than the wrestlers; then two lions, each

Right: Village devotees gather for week-long recitation of the holy book, Bhagwat Geeta, in ceremony which frees the souls of the year's departed.

as strong as 10 elephants; now two griffins each as strong as 10 lions; and finally, on the uppermost plinth, two demi-Goddesses — Baghini in the form of a tigress, and Singhini, as a lioness — each 10 times stronger than a griffin. It's a pattern of guardian sentinels found nowhere else in Nepalese temple architecture and considered significant evidence of the measure of appeasement required to placate Bhairav.

You'll need time to digest all this ambience, both exotic and enthralling, before walking on to Durbar Square to feast on its treasures which begin at its very gate, built of lime-plastered brick in the 18th century by Bhupatindra. Its arch is a depiction of the face of glory,

Kirtimukha, guarded on either side by two wooden carvings — one of Bhairav, the other of Hanuman.

The gate looks out on three remarkable temples, of different styles, whose divine proportions are concealed by all being huddled together: one, the single-storeyed Jagannath, housing an image of Harishankara; the second, a two-storeyed Krishna temple standing in front of it and housing images of Krishna, Radha, and Rukmani; and the third, the Shiva Mandir, built in the shikhara style with four porticoes each with a niche above them for plated images of gods.

Now stand here and the evening sun falls, as does the morning sun, on the north-facing Golden Gate, entrance to the Palace of 55 windows. Though more than dross, the Golden Gate, alas, is only bronze but when it catches the sun's rays it glitters and sparkles like the precious metal itself. In its artistry and its setting it's also the kind of fabled substance which story tellers like Hans Anderson would turn to golden words.

Ranjit Malla commissioned it in 1754 to adorn the outer entrance to the Taleju Temple within the Royal Palace, a one-storeyed shrine with many struts. During the Vijaya Dashami festival the Goddess is believed to take up residence in the south wing of the building.

It's an extreme example of the art work of Kathmandu Valley, regarded by many as its finest. One of the carved windows is believed to be the personal handicraft of Bhupatindra whose bronze statue — with him sitting, hands folded reverently before Taleju — faces the Golden Gate.

Each of the corners has images of Hindu goddesses, Devashri and Lakshmi, and in the temple area there's a large bell cast out of copper and iron. The temple opens its doors only once a year — between September and October — during the Dashain festival celebrations when Taleju's golden statue is placed on the back of the horse which is stabled in the courtyard and led around the town in a procession.

Opposite: Nepalese traditionally celebrate marriages during a special season. The garlanded groom is at right in traditional Nepali hat.

Right: Representation of Buddha's omnipotent, omniscient eyes gaze out from a Kathmandu stupa. Below the eyes is the symbol in the Nepalese alphabet for the figure one. Ears are never shown for Buddha disdains prayers in praise of him.

Opposite: Clad in elegant sari a pensive bride during a Nepalese wedding.

The adjacent Palace is renowned mainly for its 55-windowed Hall of Audience, an elaborately carved balcony, and its collection of priceless wood carvings, some damaged in the '34 'quake but still considered priceless. Originally built in the 15th century, the Palace was remodelled by Bhupatindra.

Again, this Durbar Square also boasts a large bell which was used both to summon worshippers and to give alarms, particularly if there was a night curfew when it was rung to send citizens scurrying home.

There are many more temples in Bhaktapur's Durbar Square — to Kumari, Vatsala, Durga, Narayan, Shiva and Pashupatinath. The last is the oldest in the city, built around the end of the 15th century by the widow and sons of King Yaksha Malla to honour his memory though some argue it was built much later, in 1682, by Jita Mall, father of Bhupatindra.

Bhaktapur legend says Lord Pashupatinath appeared before him in a dream and ordered him to build the temple. Another legend has it that the King wanted to visit the temple at Deopatan but was unable to cross the Bagmati which was in full flood and so ordered another temple to Pashupatinath to be built in Bhaktapur. The style is certainly identical and in those days a Royal wish was a command. Whatever the reason, Bhaktapur has one more treasure to guard.

It's in this ancient city that hundreds of thousands gather to celebrate the Newar New Year which falls between 13 and 16 April according to the position of the sun and moon.

Just like the rest of the world — except Ethiopia — Nepal has 365 days and 12 months in each year. But the length of the months — from 29 to 32 days long — differs, as does Nepal's first century. This began at the start of the Vikram era, the date on which King Vikramaditya of India defeated Saka in 57 BC. So Nepal is more than half a century ahead of the rest of the world.

Thus, Nepal and its citizens celebrated the dawn of the 21st century in splendid isolation. For them this auspicious event took place in April

Above: Buddhist monks at the Bodhnath stupa, near Kathmandu, throw handfuls of flour in the air during a religious festival. The largest stupa in Nepal, the worshippers are of Tibetan stock.

Opposite: Buddha's all-seeing eyes gaze down on two horn-blowing monks at the Bodhnath stupa, Kathmandu.

1943 during the time its borders remained sealed, and the rest of the world — including some brave Gurkhas — was at war. There are three other New Year Days — one based on the solar calendar and two on the lunar calendar.

Derived from the Newari words for snake, *bi*, and slaughter, *syako*, the Newar celebration is called Bisket — and therein lies another fascinating folk tale of Nepal.

On the day — during Nepal's equivalent of January, the month of Baisakh — from early in the morning, the crowds head for the Nyatapola Temple where two enormous vehicles of the gods, *raths*, with solid wooden wheels are waiting outside. Their purpose is legendary.

Long ago, Bhadra Kali, daughter of a Bhaktapur king, was so insatiable that each night he had to conscript a new man from among his citizens to serve her. None could last the pace. With reason.

Each morning the Royal stud for the night was found dead, and if not from exhaustion, inexplicably.

Now it came about that a visiting Prince, separated from his entourage, sought shelter one night in the home of a kindly old woman only to be woken soon after by the sound of sobbing. She was crying because her son had been chosen to attend the Princess the next night.

Selflessly, the Prince offered to stand in, so to speak, for the lad — arguing that by so doing he might be able to solve the mystery.

That evening, after the Princess fell into a deep and satisfied sleep, the Prince left the bed and found a place in which to hide, sword in hand.

In horror he watched, as from the Princess so fair, two threads of hair in her nostril began to emerge becoming enormous serpents, writhing

Opposite: Gilded conical canopy of the golden temple atop the 2,000 year old Swayambunath Stupa west of Kathmandu, one of the oldest Buddhist shrines in Nepal. The concentric circles represent the 13 steps needed to attain nirvana.

Above: Brightly-coloured eyes of Buddha gaze out over the Swayambhunath Stupa on the crest of a wooded hill. A shrine for more than 2,000 years it is reached by climbing 365 steps.

about seeking their nightly victim — only for the hero to pounce upon them with his sword and cut them to shreds.

All this to the surprise of the bearers who when they came in the morning expecting to carry away yet another corpse found him deep in conversation with the enraptured maiden. The King was overjoyed as, quite naturally, were the citizens — particularly the menfolk.

The snakes were draped from a tall wooden pole and the two lovers paraded around the town in their respective chariots to become husband and wife.

The victor, in fact, was Bhairav, the manifestation of Shiva in all his destructive power, and the maiden, the Goddess Bhadra Kali.

Four days before New Year her brass likeness is carried from its Bhaktapur shrine to the Nyatapola Temple and placed in the smaller of the two chariots; and Bhairav's image in the other.

Together these enormous, unwieldy vehicles are pulled through the town, up hill and down, past the Potters' Market, until they reach a spot known as Khalna Tole.

Dominating all is an 80-foot high representation of Bhairav's victorious

Left: Novice monk learning the rites of priesthood in a Kathmandu Buddhist monastery.

lingam which outwitted the serpents, draped with two banner ribbons representing the snakes, set in a massive circular four foot deep *yoni*.

It takes hours to raise the pole, a perilous occupation for often an unfortunate is killed when it comes crashing back to earth. Sometimes it refuses to stay up, an omen of evil portent for Bhaktapur which leaves everyone feeling uneasy and ready to fall out, fearful of impending disaster.

On New Year's Eve 2043 however everything goes right and the pole is there, leaning out at about 30°, and everyone is liquored-up for the occasion on a mix of marijuana, hashish and Nepal's branded and unbranded hooch.

Derring-do youths and splay-eyed adults try to best each other by shinning up the pole — or, even more perilous, up the swaying ropes — as, rib to rib on every roof top, balcony, precarious hold, and cobblestone road, with bands playing, the shadows lengthening, more than a hundred thousand people crush together to watch the climax.

Rival teams, each representing one of the deities, battle to dislodge the *lingam* and bring it crashing down. Hushed one moment, vociferous the next, the tension mounts. The *lingam's* fall — to thunderous roars and frantic flight through the tightly packed crowd as people rush to get out of its path before it crashes down in a cloud of dust — signals the death of the old year and the evil serpents.

Now more of these hyped-up contestants hurry to engage in a tug-of-war to see which wins control of Bhairav's chariot: and the right to guard the great god for the next seven days of the Bisket festival.

Heaving and straining to move the unwieldy vehicle — so heavy and vast that when its rough-hewn wheels creak you can hear the groan above the roar of the crowd — each team seeks ever more recruits to its side.

Slowly, in fits and starts of no more than a centimetre or two, to straining thighs and thews, it moves — gaining slow momentum only to come crunching to a sudden halt as all stop pulling to celebrate the juggernaut's moment of movement.

Above: An ancient pipal tree frames Nepal's first five-storeyed pagoda temple, said to have been built in 1392 by Bhaskara Deva and Amsu Varma. Famed as the winter home of Shiva, Kumbheshwar Temple takes its name from Khumba, *for pot, and* Ishwar, *for God. At left of picture is the temple dedicated to the crane-headed goddess, Baglamukhi, represented in the form of a gilded archway with a canopy of coiled snakes. Those in trouble make supplications to her for release from suffering.*

It's a combination of a world series play-off, the heavyweight championship of the world, and an international pilgrimage: New Year starts with a bang in Nepal.

Throughout the long afternoon comes the hectoring voice of the local parliamentary candidate unable to resist addressing the largest audience he will ever draw. Tourists no doubt believe his excited phrasing is a well-pitched commentary on the proceedings.

For the winners it's an auspicious omen of good fortune and a signal to celebrate the dawning of New Year even more. For the next week there'll be singing and dancing in the narrow streets with parades in honour of Brahma, Ganesh, Mahakali, Goddess of Terror, and Lakshmi.

Not just in Bhaktapur, either. Five kilometres away, the people of Thimmi mark the advent of New Year in spectacular fashion with a celebration for Bal Kumari, Thimmi's Living Goddess. All through New Year's day her temple is thronged with musicians and worshippers bringing offerings of rice, vermilion, burning oil torches, holy water, flowers and garlands for Bhairav's consort.

It's important that the four ceremonial oil torches, *chirags*, which guard

her never go out — otherwise, folk believe, Thimmi is in for a bad year!

But it's just after midnight, the start of New Year's Day, that Thimmi comes to incandescent life. Then, like gladiators of old in the streets of Rome, their route lit by torches, teams of strong young men begin to carry immensely heavy palanquins — borne on thick bamboo poles — in rowdy procession through the streets; so heavy a sudden lurch sends them all stumbling. There are 32 of these palanquins and each needs a team of 20 or 30 to carry them.

The heavy, wrought-iron little houses, like temples, *khats*, carried on these palanquins contain images of Bhaktapur's guardian deities with Kumari in principal place. It's said that the combined heat of the many torches — literally hundreds — which burn through the night and day will drive away winter and hasten summer's warmth to make their crops burgeon.

They could as well put their money on the thermal heat of the collective mass of whooping, shrieking celebrants and their supporters to achieve the same. Up and down, in endless relay, the sweating, stumbling teams, laced with rice beer and other stimulants, stagger at a

Above: Bhaktapur's Durbar Square holds matchless treasure of medieval architecture and art. At left, unmistakeable, is the Golden Gate, its gilt metal gleaming richly in the afternoon sun. Beyond it is the 15th century Palace of 55 Windows, residence of the Malla Kings, damaged in the 1934 'quake. Facing it, hands folded in reverence, is a statue of the 17th century ruler, King Bhupatindra Malla, who remodelled the Palace. Just beyond and to the right of the statue is the bell built by Ranjit Malla in 1737. And to the right of that is the shikara-styled Vatsala Temple. Below that is the bell of barking dogs. At right of that is the Square's Pashupatinath Temple, a replica of the one at Deopatan believed to have been built by Jayagita Mitra Malla in 1682 after floods prevented him reaching the temple there.

Above: Statue of King Bhupatindra Malla, hands folded reverently in deference to the family goddess, Taleju Bhawani, presides over Bhaktapur's Durbar Square.

dog-trot from one narrow cobbled street to the next, in and out around the houses, watched by many more thousands than their combined numbers.

In each group one attendant staggers with them, twirling a weighty ceremonial umbrella on a heavy bamboo pole above the deity ensconced within the *khat*, its pagoda-tiered brass roof decorated with fruit, ribbons, good-luck charms, garlands, and green shrubs.

Sun-up finds them still whooping and chanting, the balconies, windows, and rooftops, crowded with onlookers as the teams and their supporters surge through the streets below like a sea of humanity, sweeping out the unfortunate flotsam — an occasional spectator who's strayed — and jetsam — perhaps two or three panic-stricken dogs — on an irresistible tide of jubilation.

Clouds of brilliant orange-red powder hang in the air, infiltrating into hair, teeth, eyes and nose, and permeating clothing: the happiness is as infectious as the stain is ineradicable. Days later you'll still be washing the gritty red powder out of your hair. It's said to be a very special token of respect and admiration reserved only for elders, close friends and neighbours.

Crimson-red, *Simrik,* is Nepal's national colour — regarded as both sacred and auspicious, considered a symbol of progress, prosperity and action — and is predominant at all national and sacred occasions.

Climax of the mounting frenzy is when Ganesh, on a *khat* from Nagadish village — surrounded by several hundred supporters — joins the procession. Soon the rest of the palanquins join in a wild chase down the main street — nothing more than a sun-baked earth road — after Ganesh when he turns for home, to persuade him to stay and thus ensure that the celebrations continue.

The chase over, the festival moves to its colourful close with the procession moving back to the Kumari Temple, standing before the entrance to stop the Goddess's palanquin from entering — for with her departure the festival is ended.

Finally, amid much laughter, shouting and jeering, the palanquin bearers are triumphant. Bal Kumari disappears into her sanctum to rest another year while the others shoulder their deities and vanish through the thicket of lanes back to their homes.

Many carry sacrificial chickens and goats. The blood from their slit throats has already been drained and poured over the image of Bal Kumari to slake her thirst. Life's crimson ebb is precious benediction.

Today enmities and rivalry are forgotten in Thimmi. None may refuse an invitation to eat or drink. The idea is to settle scores by getting adversaries so drunk they can be left to sleep it off in the ditch or among the animal ordure which lines the streets — the host considering himself a pious victor.

But before this feasting begins the hordes form into a phalanx and head across the patchwork countryside over a series of dykes which divide their terraced fields and village from that of Bode, where each year the village elders choose a member of their community to undergo a traumatic ordeal as an act of penitence for the village. His tongue extended, a thick needle will be pierced through it by a holy man, *pujari,* and held against his lips by pressure.

Opposite: Made of gilded metal, Bhaktapur's golden gate gleams in the sun like the precious mineral itself. It was built by Ranjit Malla in 1756 and marks the entrance to the Taleju Temple within.

Above: Worshipper seeks blessings of the many gods and goddesses depicted in brass on the doorway of her local temple.

Above right: Elegantly sculptured brass detail on Vishnu temple.

Rice salesman Dil Kumar Shrestra, 25, is the chosen one. He sits cross-legged and reclusive on a mat in a small courtyard outside his house. He's been living in solitude for four days, beard, head and eyebrows shaved. His only food has been one meal a day of 'clean' food: no meat, garlic or salt. For the last 24 hours he's eaten nothing.

He smokes a cigarette. He's not afraid though his wife 'like all ladies' is fearful. The ceremony, he says, is a form of insurance so that there will be peace and health in Bode. How the tradition began he cannot remember. Neither can anybody else. All they know is that it started long ago, perhaps 300 or 400 years before.

He'd like a son who could be the penitent, too, when he grows up. It's a great honour. He looks anxious. His tongue flickers in and out in a nervous, involuntary reaction.

In Bode Square, close to where the ceremony takes place, a seven-man ensemble is beating out the rhythm on a drum, bells and anything that can add to the cacophony, like a hot combo from the roaring '20s. A procession of young virgins circles the shrine of Laxmi, Goddess of Wealth; one for each day of the week and throw rice everywhere. It's the symbol of wealth.

The crowd is thick, impossible to count: at least 50,000, several hundred of them on the frail roofs surrounding the square. The stage is a sheet of corrugated iron perched precariously on top of old packing cases and rickety chairs.

Surely it's bad theatre. But somehow it works. The drama is intense.

Kumar sits, mouth agape, while the priest inserts the needle, forged eight months earlier during the festival of Jandraganar. The needle is always new. It's been kept in oil for the last week in the Ghantakarna Temple.

Few actually see it pass through the tongue but if he bleeds it's an ill-omen, sign of Kumar's impurity during his seclusion. The gods will punish him.

Slowly, agonisingly, the needle enters the soft flesh of the tongue. The

Opposite: One of the treasures of Kahtmandu's Durbar Square: 18th century mask of Bhairav, depicting Shiva in his most ferocious aspect, made by Rana Bahadur Shah to ward off evil spirits. It plays a large part in the annual Indra Jatra festival when thousands line up behind it to siphon off litres of Jand, a sanctified rice beer, as it is poured through the grinning gargoyle mouth. The libation is considered a powerful blesing.

Above: Decorated 8th-9th century black statue of Bhairav, Shiva in his most terrifying incarnation, in Kathmandu's Durbar Square. During the Malla dynasty, people charged with crimes were taking before this demoniac sculpture. It was said that those who lied in front of the statue would bleed to death.

priest bathes the wound with oil. No blood. He pushes it deeper. Another salve. No blood.

Now he applies the final pressure. The needle breaks through. Another dab of oil. No blood.

Kumar rises, turns his body to the crowds, arms outstretched. On every side rises a thunderous roar. He is pure and truly penitent.

But his ordeal is not over. Now a giant bamboo cradle is fastened over his shoulders with about thirty smouldering oil torches.

Tongue outstretched, shoulders bowed, he walks through the village for the next 90 minutes the source of admiration for his virtue and stoic courage until, purged and purified, he enters the temple.

There the *pujari* removes the needle and cauterises the wound with mud from the temple floor. No doubt the mud is laced with tetanus and other lethal bacteria but faith is all-powerful.

No blood — and no infection!

Kumar is blessed and Bode is assured of peace and health for the next 12 months.

The memory remains vividly fresh next day as you shake yet some more of the gritty red powder out of your hair and clothes and the dust of history and Kathmandu from your feet and set out once more on Nepal's never-ending road to adventure.

Just for the fact that it lies no more than 50 kilometres from the crest of 26,398 foot high Shisha Pangma, or Gosainthan, in the west, and much the same distance from 29,028 foot high Everest, in the east, Kodari would be remarkable. But this tiny settlement is the more remarkable because it's only 5,800 feet above sea level. Even more remarkable, it's not much more than 100 kilometres from Kathmandu.

Though this short distance takes between four and five hours to cover it doesn't seem a moment too long. For this is a wonderland of raging rivers, valley towns, and forested slopes.

You set out along the the Valley highway in an early morning sun. Diffused by the soft spring haze of April it casts a golden halo over the surrounding hills. Casual brickworks dot the fields. Most buildings have their measure of this material. It's cheap, economical and durable even though the floors it supports are built of mud. But today some have floors of concrete and walls of brick from the modern — and expensive — brickworks at the end of the Valley.

There is still plenty of space between one building and the next with green paddies making good use of the land and the Valley's gentle hills looming blue-grey in the background.

Suddenly you're over the top and the road plunges several thousand feet in a series of hairpin bends: constantly used by Nepal single-decker buses turned double-deckers. Usually there are as many passengers on the roof — clearly not suffering from vertigo — as there are inside. On some bends, the bus wheels are inches from the verge — and from rooftop to Valley floor there's nothing but thousands of feet of empty space!

Like most roads in midland Nepal, this was built by the Chinese. The direct route to Lhasa, capital of Tibet, it's fairly new yet already badly damaged in sections by the frequent landslides and washaways which send whole sections of road — and sometimes the vehicles on them —

plunging to the swollen torrents below.

These tumultuous events, which wipe out roads, block canals and destroy whole villages, cause heavy losses of men and material. Not only communities can be cut off for days, so can major towns including the capital.

Valley veterans mourn the change the motor age has wrought — and is wreaking — on traditional Nepal society. Not the visitor. Before the road was built Tibet was half a world and another century away. Indeed, roads are so new in Nepal that most people — including drivers — have no traffic consciousness.

Though the Arniko Highway, *rajmarg*, winds through the foothills of the greatest mountain range in the world, these hills themselves are so high and sheer that views of the snow-capped peaks are rare. The exception is Dhulikhel at the top of the narrow ridge just below the pass out of the Valley — a thin ribbon of road with steep drops on either side — which offers a stunning vista of the Himalaya, including Everest. Apart from this, Dhulikhel is notable for the decorative and unusual wood carvings around the doors and windows of the village houses — and its three-roofed Bhagavati Temple which has a ceramic-tile facade. Far below on the valley floor the homes of low-caste Hindu peasant farmers, mud and thatch houses, and the bare red earth, are strikingly reminiscent of Africa.

Drive on, avoiding the frequent flocks of ducks and geese which cross the road, and after a few kilometres, at Dolalghat, a long low bridge crosses the wide bed of the Sun Kosi just below its confluence with the Indrawati river. It's almost half a kilometre long and the crystal clear waters, abounding with trout and other fish, are inviting in the spring sunshine.

The bridge, built in 1966, is reminder of Nepal's progress in the 35 years since it reopened its borders. Before 1955 the country boasted only 624 kilometres of road. In 1986 there were around 6,000 kilometres but the challenge is not to build roads and bridges for vehicles.

For the majority travel is by trail, footpath and suspension bridge over some of the toughest terrain in the world. Nepal has done well — more than 60 suspension bridges, for instance, were built in 1980 — linking communities which had been neighbours for years but remained as remote from each other as man on the moon.

Regularly, all along the river valleys these models of engineering curve across the gorge, evidence that Nepal is catching up fast — as witness also the new satellite ground station in Kathmandu Valley. But the charm of its antiquity remains and will do so for a long time.

Ironies abound. Not long after Dolalghat, on the Sun Kosi, is one of the country's first hydro-electric schemes, built in 1972 with Chinese aid. Two kilometres upstream, engineers are installing the first overhead power cables to connect the local communities to this 10,050 kilowatt source of energy. Nepal's first hydro-electric station was built in 1911.

With only a fraction of the world's land surface — under zero per cent — Nepal's hydro-electric potential is an impressive 2.27 per cent of world capacity.

The station lies between Lamosangu and Barabise, less than 3,000 feet above sea level and it's north of bustling Barabise that the road begins to

Opposite: Parading in long processions lit by flaming torches, all night revellers welcome New Year's Day.

Right: Vermillion powder — a token of blessing — hangs in the New Year's Day air at the advent of 2043 in April 1986. Nepal's calendar is 67 years ahead of the rest of the world but the gabled houses of wood and brick and cobbled streets have stepped straight out of the Middle Ages.

climb upwards.

All along the road the sparse winter and spring waters are tapped for irrigation and domestic use through ancient but well-kept aqueducts, models of traditional engineering dug out above the side of the streams and lined with local stone, with the fast-flowing water taken off the main body which soon descends below the level of the aqueduct. Expensive pipes and filtration processes would be costly — and would they serve better?

On the hillsides above, seemingly also suspended by faith alone, peasants carve little terraced smallholdings and till them with the

Above: Passers-by daub one of the many representations of Shiva that stand in the streets of Kathmandu and its surrounding villages with ochre-coloured tika *seeking his powerful benediction.*

Left: New Year celebrant during festivities in Kathmandu Valley.

*Above: Bode women gain a vantage point to witness
Dilip Kumar Shrestra's New Year act of penitence.*

sure-footed agility of the native goats. In the raging white waters below,
equally nimble-footed villagers plant primitive but effective fish traps of
withies and bamboo. There's much to be said for the old ways. Folk here
have long improvised civilising means.

Many visitors stop at Tatopani, one place where the villagers need
never have a cold bath. Hot springs from the raging ferment beneath the
Himalaya have been piped and the water pours forth, day and night, an
everlasting supply of running hot water.

At occasional intervals there's the inevitable temple — at Chakhu, only
15 kilometres from Tibet, there's an improbable circus pitched on a river
bank just below the edge of the road.

Eight kilometres on at Khokun a temple occupies a rock in the middle
of the gorge — with no indication of how worshippers climb up its sheer
rock faces on all sides — and a wonderful waterfall that leaps and jumps
like scintillating diamonds hundreds of feet down the sheer lush green
wall of the mountain.

The sheer rock walls of the gorge press inexorably closer and closer.
They seem to lean over the small, narrow ribbon of road which clings so

Opposite: Slender needle piercing his tongue, Dilip Kumar Shrestra begins his New Year penitence. The fact that his tongue does not bleed augurs well for Shrestra, a token of his purity during his seclusion prior to his ordeal.

precariously to the hillside. The road cuts beneath a cliff and you ask yourself what sustains such faith in the power of the rock to suspend itself indefinitely with such a mass of weight pushing down on it — and, more important, what sustains the faith of those who pass beneath?

Now you can almost reach out and touch either side of the gorge and round a bend there's a casual, desultory inquiry at the immigration post and beyond you report to the police post. One more bend and there's the border — spanned by the Friendship Bridge.

It's already the source of a thriving tourist trade. Day trippers disgorge themselves from their coach to be photographed with the Tibetan town of Khasa, 2,000 feet higher up the gorge, and the snows of 19,550 foot Choba-Bahamare beyond, in the background. To the east, directly in line with Kodari is mighty Gaurisankar, only 35 kilometres distant — but invisible beyond the rise of the gorge wall. To be so near and yet not to see this shapeliest of peaks is sadly frustrating.

A yellow line marks the middle of the bridge and, so they say, the border between China's Tibet and Nepal. In green Mao uniform, a small, non-English speaking Chinese guard steps out smartly to answer

Above: Enthralled audience hangs from Bode's rooftops and throngs the street below to witness penitent Dilip Kumar Shrestra's moment of truth: when the specially forged 25-centimetre long needle pierces his tongue. The origins of the centuries-old New Year ritual have long been lost in obscurity.

Opposite: Tongue pierced, bowed under the weight of a candelbra of flaming torches, rice salesman Dilip Kumar Shrestra undergoes a 90-minute walk of penitence through the narrow lanes of Bode village, Kathmandu.

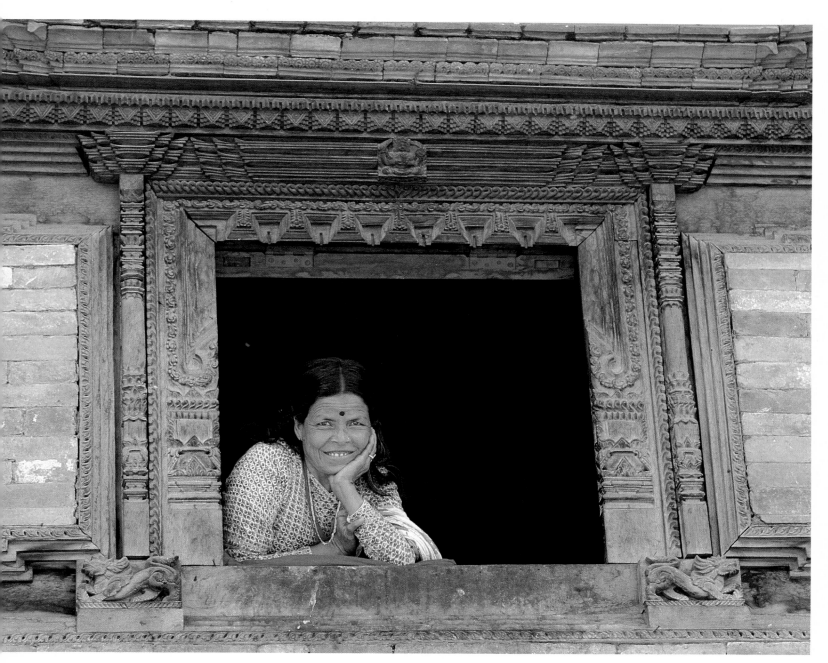

Above: Housewife smiles from the elegantly carved window of her Bhaktapur home.

incomprehensible questions from two Indian visitors from Delhi in an equally incomprehensible tongue. Whatever they want — and it turns out it's a night out up the hill in Khasa — they won't get. They have no visas.

Nepalis can cross unhindered. Visitors must get a visa — a fairly easy process — in Kathmandu. Khasa's Zhangmu Hotel is running an enviable occupancy rate on European and American guests eager to stay overnight on a two-day visa which marks the magic China immigration entry into their passport.

Where the border actually crosses — which side of the hill is Tibet or Nepal — is anybody's guess. On the other side the road winds back into what, hypothetically anyway, must be Nepal.

140

Left: Through the centuries Hindu artists carved many works on the struts and woodwork of the countless pagoda temples that dot the countryside — none more erotic than those found on the exterior of the fourth century temple at Changu Narayan.

The waters of the Bhotey Kosi rage down the gorge between with thunderous roar even though it's the dry season. It's an awesome thought to think of the Bhotey in spate during the monsoons and ice melt. Thick, strong buttress walls beneath the bridge foundations indicate the power they deflect.

Lower downstream the river broadens out, still turbulent and raging, but ideal for white-water rafting which, after mountaineering, is Nepal's premier sporting attraction, largely due to the pioneering reconnaisance of an American Al Read who carried out a systematic survey of the upstream rapids of the Trisuli and formed Nepal's first river rafting organisation. These rivers have become the Mecca of white water enthusiasts the world over.

South-west of Kathmandu, the Trisuli gorge meets that of the Mahesh Khola. From the capital to the confluence of the two rivers you take another of Nepal's major roads, the Prithvi-Tribhuvan Highway, as scenic as it is dramatic. A memorial to those who died building both

Below right: Saucy erotica on the struts of the Vishnu Temple at Changu Narayan.

Below: Erotic carving on the strut of the 1700 year old Vishnu temple at Changu Narayan.

Bottom: Detail of erotic carving on a Nepal temple.

Bottom right: Another example of Nepal's wealth of ancient temple erotica.

Highways stands at the top of the pass close to a Hindu shrine.

The pass out of the Valley leads down the almost sheer escarpment in a series of tortuous and terrifying hairpin bends. The road seems to defy gravity, hanging suspended in space. Yet farmhouses and fields are neatly kept and cultivated in this improbable landscape, some so close you could step on to the roof of a three-storey building beneath the roadside and then leap off into what seems almost certain space.

The Prithvi Highway proper begins at the town of Naubise where it leaves the older Tribhuvan Highway which turns southward to Hetauda. The building of the Prithvi Highway — in 1973 with Chinese aid — is marked at Naubise by a stone tablet set in the side of the rock wall. At times the road drops sheer to the fast-eddying waters below.

In April, though hot and muggy, the river is narrow by comparison with the snow melt and monsoon spate, its bed a tumult of giant boulders tossed down willy-nilly from above during some landslide or momentary earth tremor, which despite their size are often carried some distance during the flood season, so swift, strong and deep are these waters.

Hamlets and villages abound along the way — their one street the main highway. On the level sections on either side of the road are emerald-green rice paddies. Cultivating rice is a family affair — the men bullying the oxen teams with the ploughs, the women and children planting the young green shoots with astonishing speed and dexterity.

Paddies cling on to the mountain hundreds, and sometimes thousands, of feet above, protected from sliding away only by a fragile terrace of precious topsoil. Fields end abruptly at the edge of a gully or cliff. Many disappear in the monsoons leaving only a void where once stood half an acre of sustenance.

Where streams tumble off the cliff, lorry crews and villagers go through their early morning ablutions unconcerned by the passing traffic. Bathing is a public affair.

The most popular 'put-in' place for the Trisuli rapids — with colourful names like 'Snail's Nose' and 'Monkey Rapid' and graded from easy one to dangerous 10 on the Colorado River scale — is Charoudi, a small one-street hamlet with a wide, sandy beach where the dinghies are laid out, with paddles and life-jackets, awaiting the 0800 hour arrival of the river adventurers.

It's not just the raging torrent which the challenger has to conquer. Beneath the surface lurk deep potholes into which the current races to circle vertically in a fatal vortex. On the surface, there are deadly whirlpools. Hidden rocks and boulders just below the surface form the third potentially fatal hazard.

Drifting down the river is at first euphoric, the giant walls of the gorge seeming to disappear in the infinity of the sky; on other sections these close in so narrowly that the volume of light diminishes. There's exhilaration in the toss and bounce of the 'Tina Devi Rapids', almost placid, a minor grade two.

But now there's a more menacing roar ahead, where the gorge narrows and the road winds along a ledge a hundred feet above the river. The Gurkha crew is cautious. The dinghy is manoeuvred into the bank by a U-bend and they scamper away over the rocks to study the situation at

146

the notorious 'Up Set Rapids'. In spate it's a feared and fearsome stretch of white water and even now its thunder is filled with menace.

They run back, lithe, fit and fearless. The dinghy is pushed off and bounces into the main stream, racing around the bend. Ahead the water boils and crashes over the rocks.

The leader screams a battle cry. The paddles dig deep into the foaming river as the dinghy is caught and tossed like a frail matchstick and the waters roar in over the side.

Newcomers bounce into the middle of the dinghy caught in a kind of heart-pounding trance, adrenaline flowing, as the dinghy dips into a deep and powerful pothole and miraculously bounces out clear of the spray and suddenly it's in the powerful but calm swirl of the current downstream. The crew let loose an exultant victory scream. Exhilaration returns.

In a rare tragedy three months before, the crew lost one of their colleagues, downstream at the Mugling Rapid, when the current tossed him overboard into a pothole. He had no life jacket and his body did not surface until three days later. River rafting can be deadly. But usually it's

Above: Young Gurung child and buffalo in the hill village of Bhichor. The Gurung community totals more than quarter of a million and their language is a mixture of Tibetan and Burmese.

Above: Smiling schoolgirl carries home water in a brass urn.

tremendous fun.

There's a picnic lunch just before the next rapids, called the 'Surprise'! Afterwards they arrow through the narrow cleft between the foam-battered rocks with an ease born of experience.

Most rafting expeditions take two or three days to cover the Trisuli, down beyond the raging Mugling rapids, under the elegant Jholunge Pul suspension bridge, and on to Chitwan.

An optional end however is to leave the river at Mugling and travel along the Prithvi Highway to the magic valley of Pokhara. Not long after Mugling there's a northward turn off the Highway which takes you to Gorkha, the ancestral seat of the Shah dynasty, rulers of Nepal since the 18th century.

King Prithvi Narayan Shah's old Palace still stands on a mountain ridge overlooking this ancient capital from which the Gurkha soldiers derive their name. There are some famous and distinctive temples in the town including the pagoda style Manakamana dedicated to a Hindu deity with the power to make dreams come true.

During the clear season there are stunning views of Annapurna and its sister mountains from Gorkha but nothing beats the panorama which greets you in Pokhara with the mirror reflection of the sacred Machhapuchhare shining in the still, crystal waters of Phewa Lake. And Annapurna and its surrounding peaks stand up clear, just 50 kilometres from the village street which at 3,000 feet above sea level is 23,545 foot beneath the peak of Annapurna I.

Like Kathmandu, Pokhara Valley is blessed with fertile soil and with an average of more than 155 inches of rain a year this land burgeons with lush vegetation: bananas, cacti, rice, citrus trees, mustard fields, bounded with hedges of thorny spurge spiked with red blossoms, walls studded with ficus.

The patchwork terraces are cut through by gorges channelled by the Seti river and studded with lakes that glitter like diamonds in the spring sunshine. The ochre mud-and-thatch homes of the Hindu migrants from the Terai contrast to the white-walled, slate-roofed homes of the native Lamaistic tribes from the flanks of the mountain.

Thirty years ago, Pokhara was an insignificant, little-known town, an anachronism even in ancient Nepal. The first motor vehicle, a Jeep, arrived in 1958 — by plane.

Progress since then, encouraged by tourists and climbers, the advent of hydro-electric power in 1967 and the completion of the Prithvi Highway in 1973, has been swift. Within a decade Pokhara's population doubled to 50,000. There's even a movie house and amusement park now.

The indigenous people have become submerged in the tide of Manang entrepreneurs, Tibetan refugees and Gurkha soldiers who now claim the place as their own. It is here that British Gurkha pensioners straggle down from the mountainsides for their monthly pensions of a few pounds.

Local legend says Lake Phewa covers an ancient city which was engulfed with water during a cataclysmic earthquake millennia ago. Today local fishermen ply their long dug-out canoes, fashioned from tree trunks, on the placid waters, ferrying pilgrims to the shrine of Vahari, a

Left: Rafting expedition prepares for a ride down the white waters of the Trisuli River.

golden temple nestling on an island. There's also a Royal Palace for winters on the lake shore.

Barley, wheat, millet, rice and maize are grown in the valleys that lie between the mountains. Slashes of brilliant orange or white mark the farms of the Brahmins, Chhetris, Gurungs and Magars who tend the fields, their gardens filled with the colours of poinsettias, marigolds and other flowers and shady banyan trees.

The people of the Manang Valley however are famous for their trading. Tibetan in culture, they travel to many parts of the orient, Singapore, Hong Kong, and Bangkok, to do business.

Another trading community is that of the Thakali people whose colourful trade caravans of mules, loaded with sugar, kerosene, and rice, travel through the low-lying Kali Gandaki gorge, one of the most important trade routes for centuries between Tibet and Nepal and India and the deepest gorge in the world. Like the Manang community their settlements are distinguished by the flat roofs of their houses.

There are many places of pilgrimage in these hills that line the Kali Gandaki basin: Muktinah at 12,460 feet, where an eternal flame burns drawing Hindu and Buddhist alike. Black ammonite fossils, thought of as the embodiment of Vishnu, are also found in profusion and pilgrims travel long distances over rugged trails to collect these.

Everywhere the hills are lined with forests of rhododendron, azalea and bamboo except in the rain shadow where the land is sere and barren. And by the side of every trail, rippling streams dance down the hillside, their babbling song a celebration of nature's marvels.

The Gorge is flanked on one side by the daunting massif of Annapurna and only 35 kilometres away on the other side stands 26,795 foot high Dhaulagiri — and in between, almost five miles below at only 3,900 feet, sits the village of Tatopani.

Yet for all this it is Machhapuchhare that dominates every vista in Pokhara: its twin peaks, twisted like a fish's tail, standing in divine solitude.

To the west of Pokhara is a small village which is the gateway to the Royal Dhorpotan Hunting Reserve. South-west of this enchanted valley

Overleaf: Crew of a Lama Excursions white-water expedition speed through 'Surprise' Rapids on the Trisuli River below Chanaudi on the Prithvi Highway from Kathmandu to Mugling. Nepal has some of the most exciting white-water rivers in the world, graded one to seven on the Colorado River scale.

lies Baglung — reachable only by foot or dubious road from the Terai. Hand-made paper is its most famous product, used for packing and bamboo crafts. It's the home of the Thakalis, a small group of no more more than 20,000 people of Tibetan-Mongoloid stock whose faith is a mixture of Buddhism, Hinduism, and Bonpo, who speak a Tibetan-Burman vernacular.

It also earns praise from the impotent and those on the wane for the power of a local aphrodisiac — 'Silajit'. Locals travel far north to exploit deposits of this tar-like substance that oozes from rocks and fetches high prices in India.

Aesthetically produced crafts include woollen blankets, vests, rugs, and other sewn or woven handicrafts. But Baglung prospers most as a link, a trade gateway, with the ancient, forgotten kingdom of Mustang.

After Baglung you're deep into Nepal's mystical west: closed, barred and still little known. Yet it once nurtured a great kingdom of the Mallas which reached its height in the 14th century.

On the map the capital of this ancient kingdom is marked as Jumla, set almost 8,000 feet above sea level, and reached only — unless you're an untiring trekker prepared to go for weeks — by plane. Consequently, though there's a scheduled air service to Jumla — subject, of course, to weather and other vagaries — there are few visitors to this region.

For those who appreciate the uncorrupted and undisturbed, who still hope that a corner of the world may remain as life fashioned it centuries ago, this may be no bad thing.

Ringed by magnificent peaks, Jumla is truly a natural paradise, a quaint rural town with a bazaar, lined by the flat-roofed houses of the region and boasting no more than 50 shops, a bank, police station and the inevitable tea houses.

The Mallas ruled a land of rugged beauty — high open valleys demarcated by the long ridgebacks of the Himalaya, and punctuated by thick stands of forest and sparkling alpine meadows with springtime

Above: Placid waters of Lake Phewa at Pokhara in the shadows of Annapurna provide bounteous yield of fish for the local community and a shrine for pilgrims — the small golden temple of Vahari — on an island at its centre.

Overleaf: Divine 'fish-tail' peaks of sacred Machhapuchhare rise above a halo of cloud, north-west of Pokhara. Early in the 1950s, a British expedition which climbed to within 500 feet of the summit, suggested that at least one major Nepal peak should remain forever undefiled by man. No more expeditions have been allowed on the mountain.

carpets of dainty wild flowers.

The Mallas kept a winter capital at Dullu in the south of the Mahabharat Lekh range of hills and maintained a territory that stretched from the humid Terai to the Taklahar in Western Tibet — over trails that even today few tackle. Yet they left a magnificent legacy in Jumla: sculptured temples, stone pillars and the still-living folk songs of the region.

But this beauty is well-guarded. Few disturb its tranquility and population is sparse. The Karnali Zone — one of 14 in Nepal — has a total population of around 300,000: no more than 12 people to every square kilometre.

So make the most of its pristine wilderness while it remains.

There's an old highway along the Tila Nadi valley where you measure your pace by the distance between the ancient milestones placed here as long ago as the 15th century. Two days hard slog bring reward — a refreshing dip in the hot springs at Seraduska.

Walk east for three days and you'll reach Gothichaur — an alpine valley set more than 9,500 feet above sea level flanked by pine forests with a stone shrine and a water spout, legacy of the Malla dynasty, together with stupendous views of two little-known peaks, Chyakure Lekh and Patrasi Himal. Jumla is also the stepping off point for a long, hard trek to the *Shangri-la* Valley of Humla.

Best of all, make the four-day trek over high passes like Padmara, Bumra and the 11,341 foot high Ghurchi Pass and finally Pina to Rara, Nepal's most enchanting national Park, which includes Lake Rara, the Kingdom of Nepal's largest sheet of water, covering 10 square kilometres almost 10,000 feet above sea level. Snow lingers here as late as May and June but its crystal-blue waters are haven to a treasury of hardy avian visitors, particularly mallards, pochards, grebes, teals and other species, from the north.

The Park itself covers 104 square kilometres. Alpine meadows line the lake shores and fields of millet and wheat are flanked by pine forests. There is potential for apple orchards — one tree will yield around 2,500 apples a year — and the lake waters are rich with fish. Several villages stand on its shores, their houses terraced like the land, backed on to steep hillsides.

Wildlife includes hordes of impudent monkeys who raid farms and grain stores with seeming impunity. Set like a sapphire in its Himalaya amphitheatre, Lake Rara is both a botanical and faunal treasury.

There's another National Park, Dolpo, several days distant, south-west of Rara — Khaptad at much the same elevation and covering 187 square kilometres: a floral repository of high-altitude conifers, oak and rhododendron forests, its open meadows reserved for Royalty.

West lie more little-known valleys reached only on foot and south, too, the trade caravans — even goats and sheep are used as pack animals — must travel daunting distances over forbidding terrain before reaching the temperate and fertile lands of the Mahabharat and the tropical fields of the Terai.

This remoteness and timelessness would make this least-known aspect of a *Journey through Nepal* the most fascinating but for one thing: the Himalaya, the most majestic mountains in the world.

4. *The Mountains and the Monasteries*

The Himalaya rise where once was a sea. Flying towards them from the west, in the jet stream at 30,000 feet, the Indian plains beneath are sere — parched and barren, a spread of stunted brown. A ridge of cotton wool clouds to the north, shadowed by a mass of brooding, anvil-shaped cumulonimbus, begins to draw near.

Jagged peaks, some black and fearsome like hidden rocks, others ice-white, lurk within. Occasionally, there's a break in the fortress-like ramparts — one of the few passes through the almost impenetrable Roof of the World. Elsewhere, the clouds billow, like white caps on the ocean, and comb over to break on the rocky shores of this reef in the sky.

At wing-tip level, east and west, the panorama stretches as far as the eye can see. Looking down it seems impossible that anyone, or anything, could live within the frozen embrace of these peaks. Yet, locked in a hundred secret valleys, reached only by fragile footpaths sometimes carved out of the side of a sheer rock face thousands of feet above a rocky river gorge, the cultural wealth of Nepal's mountain communities and tiny, forgotten kingdoms is beyond value.

As mountains go, the Himalaya are young. The peak of Everest, which shreds the jet stream at 29,028 feet, is made of marine rock of the Cretaceous age which formed the bed of the Tethys Sea when it ebbed and flowed here 80 to 60 million years ago. Then, grinding and crunching, the Indian island met the Asian continent at the end of the Mesozoic era: the tremendous pressure of weight forcing up the bed of the Tethys Sea, foot by foot, until it tipped the sky.

On Nepal's western border, the Himalaya curve southward, like a scimitar, enfolding the country and dividing it physically from the northernmost reaches of India. The highest of these western peaks is Api.

Though small by comparison with its sister peaks in central and eastern Nepal, few mountains in the world except those in Asia rise as high as Api's 23,399 feet, forming a formidable massif in the far west. Peak to peak, directly in line with Api, only 60 kilometres away is its easterly neighbour, Saipal, just 319 feet lower. The actual border is marked by the Kali River which flows down below lonely Api.

Api dominates a range of magnificent but rarely seen and little-known peaks including Jetibohurani, 22,470 feet, Bobaye, 22,337 feet, Nampa, 22,164 feet and Rokapi, 21,218 feet. Close to Saipal stands the jagged peak of Firnkopf West touching 21,930 feet and northward is lonely Takpu Himal which gazes down on the lovely Humla valley and its remote capital of Simikotat from 21,769 feet.

Minnows compared to the peaks of central and eastern Nepal, these mountains remain relatively untouched by climbers. Japanese teams conquered Api in 1960, Saipal in 1963 and Nampa in 1972.

A major trade route from the plains, a long trek through tough country, winds between these two massifs cresting a saddle of more than 18,000 feet between Nampa and Firnkopf West before entering Tibet over the Urai Pass.

Nepal's wildlife — free from molestation or pressures for land from swift-gowing human populations — flourishes in these remote highland areas. Musk deer, bears and other species roam here and there's the delightful Red Panda. This diminutive creature, also known as the red

Above: Dry bed of a river cuts through the Suikhet Valley far below, as women carrying heavy loads of building stone make their way to the village of Dhampus.

Overleaf: Verdant rice field north of Pokhara, with the pyramid peak of sacred Machhapuchhare rising 22,944 foot above sea level. At right are Annapurna IV, 24,688 feet high, and Annapurna II, 26,041 feet high. Extreme right is 22,921 foot high Lamjung.

cat bear, a relic of a long gone era from the age of the rhinoceros, which walks like a bear and spits like a cat, is threatened with extinction.

Not much more than two feet from claw to shoulder with a 40-centimetre long tail, coloured with bright chestnut rings, its glossy fur glows with a rich rufous sheen. The face is cat-like and although it has claws similar to a bear, like a cat it can partially retract them.

It lives in temperate forests up to a height of 12,000 feet and is mainly arboreal, doing little on the ground. Red pandas, hunted for their pelts which fetch high prices in India, make delightful pets.

Eastwards of the remote western regions the Himalaya climb steadily higher. In the little-known Kanjiroba Himal, a cluster of mountains which takes its name from the highest peak, 11 peaks rise above 20,000 feet including 22,583 foot high Kanjiroba Himal. The mountains encircle the ancient Kingdom of Dolpo and the sacred Crystal Mountain, forming the natural boundaries of the Shey-Phoksondo National Park. Dolpo came into the Kingdom in the 18th century as a result of King Bahadur Shah's conquests.

Undisturbed, the Park's 3,540 square kilometres of alpine forests and meadows and cloud-wreathed ice peaks, are notable for blue sheep, yak, wild dog, brown bear, muntjac, musk deer, goral, thar and elusive snow leopard.

Bird life is rich, too, with the snow partridge, snow cock, yellow-billed chough, Blood pheasant and Tibetan twite among the endemic species.

Nepal's wild sheep, like the Great Tibetan Sheep, and the Blue Sheep, are prized trophies: thus their numbers are diminishing despite the strict controls imposed by the wildlife authorities, difficult to enforce in such isolated and rugged regions as Shey-Phoksondo National Park.

The Blue Sheep has particularly impressive horns. Rams have a black face and chest but the general body of both male and female blends well with the slate-blue shale of Dolpo where they favour open grassy slopes

between the 12,000 and 16,000 foot contours.

Largest of all Nepal's wild sheep, the Great Tibetan Sheep is diminishing fast through poaching, hunting and encroachment on its normal environment. Its horns are broad, corrugated and dramatically curved in the male. Generally a shaggy-looking grey, it lives above 16,000 feet in summer, descending to more sheltered slopes in winter.

The Himalayan thar is a superb species of mountain goat which clings to precipitious cliff faces. Reddish-brown in colour, the long, lean head with erect ears forms a lovely profile. The November to January rutting season is spectacular for the fights between rival males which sends many crashing down the cliff face to their doom. Only the strongest and most sure-footed will mate.

Strangely, the goral — described as a goat antelope by Himalayan wildlife authority Dr. Tej Kumar Shrestha — is common and remains unmolested. Or perhaps not so strangely since it offers little for the trophy hunter.

If wildlife is to survive anywhere in Nepal it will be these alpine species in such places as the magic valley of Dolpo. Walking through one of the thick forests, along the lower slopes of a river gorge, it's sometimes possible to see a rare flash of another threatened species: the muntjac — or barking deer. Or, even rarer, perhaps frozen in the dappled sunlight of a glade in the thickets, the startled look of the musk deer.

Its numbers have dropped steeply in the last decade — hunted ruthlessly for its musk pod, despite its place in Hindu religious scriptures. Renowned for its lithe grace and beauty, it is well adapted for its mountain environment, sure-footed and agile, able to leap and run over the most precipitous slopes.

Its hooves have evolved to enable it to keep up a swift pace even on ledges along a narrow cliff but it has no antlers. Reaching just over three feet at the shoulder, the hindquarter is slightly higher which enables it to run more swiftly and jump more powerfully. As it ages, the deer's dappled coat changes to yellowish-brown. Its musk is highly prized for perfumes and medicines.

Yet Dolpo will never be a tourist retreat. From the nearest road, it takes three weeks of tough walking to reach Dolpo and its monasteries which straggle up the pitch of long and tortuous ridges, above an expanse of rumpled, brown and barren mountains.

Here, as it did 15 centuries ago, the creed of the Shaman — spirit-possessed holy men — still runs strong. Spirits with names like 'Warrior King of the Black Crag' and 'Great Lord of the Soil God' and 'Fierce Red Spirit' are invoked from the shadows of eternity to take hold of the Shaman to exorcise those who are plagued by bad luck and ill-omen.

Convulsive shaking, during a ceremony known as *puja*, is the key sign of possession. If the Shaman cannot find the lost soul of the patient he will die.

In the rarefied air of these 10,000 to 16,000 foot heights perceptions and sensations are acute. Sitting atop a mountain ridge in the dark night in a yak-hair tent, wind howling, rain lashing down, watching the Shaman as he is taken hold of by 'Fierce Red Spirit with the gift of the life force of seven black wolves' is enough to convince even the most cynical witness from western civilization of the power of the supernatural.

Above: Baby on back, a mother prepares the family supper uncaring of the falling rain.

Above: Young toddler hangs in basket from a Tolkha Valley farmhouse near Pokhara.

The few hundred Dolpos who herd their yaks and goats in these sterile climes, where they also grow wheat, barley and potatoes in stony fields, are Laimaist Buddhists who speak a Tibetan dialect, mainly traders who use pack beasts to move their goods in caravans from Tibet to the more populous areas of Nepal. They ride tough highland ponies and are adept horsemen. The numbers of locals have been swollen by Tibetan refugees. All make votive offerings, some of tablets of clay and funeral ash delicately carved with a pantheon of Buddhist deities.

At a height of more than 13,000 feet, Dolpo's grain fields are among the highest cultivated land in the world. The paths and trails which lead through this tiny principality of old are often no more than shale strata sticking out of a sheer cliff face. With a sheer drop inches away on one side as you stoop low under an overhang it's only for the brave or agile.

This is a land of holy peaks of which the most revered is the Valley's sacred Crystal Mountain. According to local legend, a thousand years ago a Tibetan ascetic, Drutob Senge Yeshe, flew to the top of the harsh slab of rock, a massif that rises out of the shale around it, aboard a magic snow lion, challenged the god who lived there, and when he defeated him the rock turned to crystal.

Now Dolpo people circle the 16-kilometre circumference of the mountain's base in an annual pilgrimage known as *kora*. Its many strata — layers of rock — also draw pilgrims of a different faith: geologists hunting for fossil samples.

But it's the elusive and threatened snow leopard not the mythical snow lion which has made Dolpo a more recent centre of study. The least known and most impressive of the big cats is still shrouded in mystery and legend. Wildlife writer and zoologist George B. Schaller described the 'imperilled Phantom of the Asian Peaks' from observations in Pakistan in the late 1960s and Peter Mathiesen wrote a fascinating book, *The Snow Leopard*.

The snow leopard's range stretches more than 3,000 kilometres — the length of the Himalaya — from the far east end of the range to the borders of Afghanistan in the west.

Zoological specimens — fewer than 100 — are rare and, as Schaller says, the cat's 'luxurious smoky-gray coat, sprinkled with black, both protects and imperils the snow leopard. It permits it to fade into rocky backgrounds, but its magnificence arouses man's greed.'

The cats' main prey is the Blue Sheep and for this reason Shey-Phoksondo National Park is one of the few places where they can be studied in the wild. Their range of territory extends to great heights but they normally live in rock and forest between the 10,000 and 14,000 foot contours.

Snow leopards, known as Hiun Chituwa in Nepali, are smaller than the common leopard, just over a metre from muzzle to rump with a long and slender tail of about equal length. They breed in the winter and spring, between January and May, often living close to one another and following common trails but tending nonetheless to remain solitary.

In Dolpo.they have come perilously close to extinction, hunted by poachers armed with poisoned spears: planted in traps along riversides and rocky passes known to be used by the animals for though they have an extensive territorial range — often occupying 160 square kilometres —

they return frequently to their preferred area. Even a superficial wound is lethal.

It's more than a snow leopard's leap north-east from Shey-Phoksondo, across the forbidding perils of the 21,326 foot barrier of Hanging Glacier Peak, but for those who make the long trek there's fascinating reward. Once over the pass, they should be able to look and behold, Lo!

Dolpo's neighbouring kingdom is where myth and fantasy seem stronger than reality: a lunar land of canyons and ridges dominated by the fortress walls of a town plucked out of a book by Tolkien. The town's central feature is a massive white-walled Royal Palace in which lives the world's least-known monarch.

Time barely moves in feudal Lo. In the capital, Mantang, schools are bringing change. But while the youngsters come home filled with stories of space flights which they've heard on the classroom transistor, their grandparents still believe the world is flat and shaped like a half moon.

Lo Mantang, in fact, is the full name of the 2,000 square kilometre kingdom of His Highness King Jigme Parwal Bista, founded in the 14th century by the Tibetan warlord Ama Pal. It lies on a barren valley floor at around 15,000 feet, snug against the Tibetan border on three sides and guarded by formidable 24,000 foot high mountains, pierced only by narrow passes. On the Nepal side, massive Dhaulagiri, at 26,795 feet the world's seventh highest mountain, provides the defence which has sealed Lo from the outside world through the centuries.

Fabled Mustang, as it's now known on the maps, is only an 'honorary' kingdom these days but each night King Jigme, the 26th monarch since the 1480s, orders the only gate of the mud-walled capital shut and barred to keep out invaders or intruders. Twelve dukes, 60 monks, 152 families and eight witches occupy the capital.

King Jigme still owns serfs who plough his stony fields for grain crops.

Above: Royal Nepal Airlines Twin Otter prepares to launch itself from the cliff top runway at Lukla, perched at 9,200 feet above sea level in the Himalaya foothills. The 40-minute flight covers a road journey of 10 days and is the first stage of the eight-day trek to the Everest base camp and beyond.

Above: Game of volleyball for high-altitude rangers at the Sagamartha National Park headquarters — 11,500 feet above sea level.

But Lo's treasures are many and priceless: a wealth of Tibetan art, monasteries and forts in its 23 villages and two other towns. Many of Mustang's monasteries — the name derives from the Tibetan phrase 'plain of prayer', *Mon Thang* — are carved into cliff faces. You climb a ladder to reach them.

Other wealth lies in the rocky hills: turquoise and rich deposits of alluvial gold on the beds of the rivers that course through the land. But Lo's citizens consider the task of panning for this metal beneath their dignity.

The King's subjects — Lopas who are Laimist Buddhists — number around 8,000 and speak their own dialect of the Tibetan language. The women practise polyandry — often marrying two or three brothers!

He keeps his authority as a ruler by virtue of a 160-year-old treaty to King Birendra Shah's dynasty and payment to Nepal of 886 rupees a year and one horse. In return he holds the rank of Colonel in the Nepalese Army.

So archaic is the kingdom, matches were unknown until a few years ago and superstitious fears are rampant. The whole land goes to bed in terror of Lo's 416 demons of land, sky, fire and water and life is dedicated to warding off the evil spirits which can cause Lo's 1,080 known diseases as well as five forms of violent death.

Thus King Jigme's subjects celebrate New Year for three days each year by 'chasing the demons': with the noise of cymbals, drums, and notes made by playing on human skulls, filling the air.

Not a single tree grows in this arid and withered land. To supplement their monotonous diet of Yak milk and sour cheese they nurture fragile gardens.

For trade, the Lopas deal in salt from Tibet. One of the trails they follow winds for 240 kilometres along the Kali Gandaki Gorge between

Opposite: Neat Sherpa houses climb the hillside at Namche Bazaar beneath Khumde's icy peak.

Overleaf: Sagamartha National Park headquarters at Josare, above Namche Bazaar, looking south down the Monjo Valley.

165

two of the world's great mountains. For with Dhaulagiri and Annapurna you have come to the frontier of the highest land in the world.

Here, and farther to the east, is where men measure their mettle midst these majestic monoliths — and sometimes die in the testing. No wonder. Within a length of 500 kilometres (just under two-thirds of the distance between Nepal's east-west borders) and within a breadth of 70 kilometres from south to north, no fewer than 138 peaks rise above 20,000 feet.

Dhaulagiri Himal has 14 major peaks above 21,000 feet, six of them alone on the Dhaulagiri massif, of which the smallest is almost 24,000 feet. No more than 50 kilometres distant, Annapurna Himal boasts 21 peaks of which the smallest, Gyaji Kang, has yet to be surveyed. The 20th peak, Pheri Himal, touches 20,243 feet and and 18 rise above 21,000 feet.

Beyond this, just 70 kilometres east, lies Manaslu Himal with 12 peaks above 21,000 feet; 110 kilometres east of that, Langtang Himal's 24 major peaks all rise above 20,000 feet; and another 70 kilometres on Rolwaling Himal's 17 peaks all top 21,500 feet.

Move another 50 kilometres and Mahalangur Himal, in the Khumbu region, and Khumbu Himal boast a total of 26 peaks all above 21,000 feet between them including Everest at 29,028 feet; and finally, just another 130 kilometres away at 28,208 feet, the world's third highest mountain, Kanchenjunga, dominates 24 sister peaks all above 22,000 feet.

Not surprisingly there aren't many patrols along the Tibet-Nepal and Nepal-India borders. Nor is it any surprise to learn that there are hundreds of mountains in Nepal under 20,000 feet — and some above that height — which have yet to be named.

Before 1950 these peaks were shrouded in mystery, virtually unknown except those which could be reached from the Tibetan side from which all the early assaults on Everest were made. Even today the Nepalese rule which peak or not may be challenged: only 122 major mountain peaks are open to foreign climbers. The rest, many of them regarded as holy or sacred, remain inviolate.

The mystique of mountain climbing has never been rationalised. The risks are incalculable — an average of one out of every 40 climbers who ascend the major Himalaya peaks never returns — and success achieves nothing of a scientific or creative nature.

George Mallory, who vanished with his companion Andrew Irvine during a 1925 attempt on Everest from the Tibetan side, explained his reason for putting his life on the line simply: 'Because it's there.'

Is that why men take the unforgiving risk? Perhaps so.

In 1981 Joe Tasker wrote of climbing in the Himalaya, in his book, *Everest the Cruel Way*:

'...the mountains are never conquered; they will always remain and sometimes they will take away our friends if not ourselves. The climbing game is a folly, taken more or less seriously, an indulgence in an activity which is of no demonstrable benefit to anyone. It used to be that mountaineers sought to give credence to their wish to climb mountains by concealing their aims behind a shield of scientific research. But no more. It is now accepted, though not understood, that people are going to climb for its own sake.'

A year later Tasker was dead: killed with his colleague Peter Boardman on the north-east ridge of Everest — which claimed Mallory and Irvine — in an expedition led by Chris Bonnington.

Later, in a 1985 expedition on the same face, climber Sandy Allan, quoted in Andrew Greig's *Kingdoms of Experience*, soliloquised: 'Here, we're here, I'm here, hoping that my ability and the rest of the lads' ability and the gods will see us OK. We're gamblers, we've got no cash; we have lives, we love them, that's the stake.'

He and Tasker were driven by the same passions and dreams as the greatest mountaineer of all, Italian Reinhold Messner, who made his first visit to the Himalaya in 1970: a need to measure himself, a need to be first. If he failed, he was not found wanting.

Like the poles, the greatest heights on earth have always lured the brave and the reckless. Before 1950 no man had been known to reach the summit of a mountain which stood above the magic 8,000 metres — 26,250 feet — mark: though Mallory and Irvine who vanished on Everest may have actually reached the summit.

When Nepal opened its doors to foreigners in 1950 the first to venture into its hidden mountain sanctuaries were British climbers Eric Shipton and H.W. Tilman who 'discovered' the Langtang Himal's many marvels — just 75 kilometres north of Kathmandu — unknown then to many Nepalese.

But it was Frenchman Maurice Herzog and his team which were given the first permit to tackle Nepal's giants — Dhaulagiri and Annapurna — and on 3 March 1950, as Shipton and Tilman toiled through the upper reaches of the Langtang Valley astounded at the size and beauty of its towering peaks and precipices, Herzog and his colleague Louis Lachenal crested the brow of Annapurna's north face and looked down from the 26,545 foot high peak of the world's 10th highest mountain: the first men ever to do so.

At once Annapurna exacted vengeance. The French pair, descending in appalling weather, lost fingers and toes from frostbite. Unforgiving

Above: Sherpa woman walks by shrine-topped Buddhist stupa above Namche Bazaar. A thin veil of snow covers the craggy peaks of 19,300 foot high Khumbila in background.

Opposite: The 22,444 foot high peak of Ama Dablam shyly shows its crown above the bend on the precipitous mountain trail from Namche Bazaar to Everest View Hotel as yak pack beasts carry trekkers' equipment to the next camp.

and vengeful, this 'Goddess of Plenty' has reaped terrible retribution since: by the end of 1984 it had claimed a total of 31 lives — one for each person who had reached its summit — a figure exceeded only by those lost on Everest. Though seemingly benign and benevolent when viewed from Pokhara early on a spring day, Annapurna is baleful and malevolent.

There's more than just a touch of fancy to the sensations and emotions climbers experience at extremely high altitude. Above 8,000 metres, after all, they are intruding into the 'Abode of the Gods' where mysticism prevails over cynicism.

Reinhold Messner, in solitude on the peaks of major mountains, has experienced this mysticism frequently. During his 1982 solo ascent of Kanchenjunga his perception was profound. 'First, I learned in dreams during the climb and afterwards — and this is true only for climbs of mountains higher than 8,000 metres — the whole dream world changes for a while...

'And second, I found that you see certain things between dreaming and not dreaming because you don't really sleep...I'm quite sure that many *lamas* [Buddhist priests] have visions from high altitudes...In the last camp near the summit, I had a very strange vision of all the human parts I am made of...not only of my body, but of my whole being.'

When Herzog and Lachenal looked down Annapurna's sheer South Face they judged it unclimbable. Yet 20 years later a British expedition led by Chris Bonnington, Don Whillans and Dougal Haston achieved the 'impossible'.

During the final leg to the summit, Haston experienced something of the acute awareness which Messner records. Going down the fixed ropes after reaching the peak, Haston suddenly went into a state of total euphoria as he explains very simply in Bonnington's book, *Annapurna, South Face*: 'Everything seemed beautiful. Inside and out.'

The euphoria was short-lived. When Bonnington, who was at the 20,100 foot high Camp III, heard news of the triumph he wanted to pull everybody off the mountain immediately. 'There was,' he writes, 'a feeling of indefinable menace in the air. It was as if the whole mountain was ready to reject us, as if we were tiny foreign bodies or parasites clinging to a huge, living organism, whose automatic defensive mechanism had at last come to life.'

Whillans shared these feelings. When the two reached Camp III Whillans, a hard-bitten, taciturn Yorkshireman, told Bonnington: 'You want to get everyone off the mountain as quickly as possible. It's falling apart. The whole place feels hostile somehow.'

Added Bonnington: 'The strange thing was that the lower one got down the mountain, the more dangerous it felt...' The foreboding was justified. Only hours later Ian Clough, descending with two other members, was buried under an avalanche and killed instantly.

These avalanches pose as great a threat to climbers as falls. Annapurna with its three other peaks — II at 26,146 feet, III at 24,787 feet, and IV at 24,688 feet — is particularly hazardous. Avalanches thunder down the slopes almost by the hour just before and during the monsoon season.

Women are as prone to the fascination of mountain climbing as men and Annapurna draws no distinctions. Two members of a 1978 American

Overleaf: Angry clouds boil and billow around the
crumpled flanks of 21,130 foot high Cholatse in
Sagamartha National Park as trekkers negotiate ice-
field and moraine on stamina-sapping walk to 17,560
foot high Gokyo.

Above: Seen across the Ngojumba Glacier on a cloudless morning, 25,990 foot high Gyachunk Kang stands serene, belying the frequent tempests which shroud its knife-edge peak in cloud and storm.

women's expedition — Vera Watson and Alison Chadwick-Onyszkiewicz — fell 1,500 feet to their deaths at a height of around 24,000 feet. They are among a number of brave women who have met their deaths on the ice-cliffs of the Himalaya.

Since the 1970s climbing techniques have changed. All these earlier expeditions — Bonnington's 1970 Expedition was on Annapurna for 10 weeks — employed what amounted to seige tactics: establishing a base camp and then a series of camps higher and higher up the mountainside from which to launch an assault on the summit.

The organisation and logistics involved in mounting such an expedition are impressive. Bonnington led a team of 10 world-class climbers to Annapurna — backed up by a small army of porters and Sherpa climbers. The expedition which set off from Pokhara on 22 March 1970 contained more than 160 people.

Sponsors had to be found, supplies shipped across the world and then across India and, in addition, Bonnington had to organise liaison and delivery of news film to Britain's Independent Television News service — it was the first expedition ever filmed for television — from his mountain fastness to Pokhara, on to Kathmandu and then London.

Nepal's Ministry of Tourism exercises strict control over the number of expeditions to the mountains which, after Everest the most popular, include Kanchenjunga, Lhotse, Makalu, Dhaulagiri, Manaslu, Annapurna and — since 1981 -- Cho Oyu. Permission has to be obtained years in advance. In 1983, for instance, the Ministry knew which expeditions would be climbing Everest in 1988.

There's gold in them thar' hills. Each expedition pays the government a royalty fee. To stand on top of Everest costs 15,000 rupees: all the other 8,000 metre peaks are valued at 14,000 rupees. Each expedition must employ a Government liaison officer at base camp and only Nepalese can work as high-altitude guides and porters. But the daily rates for such

Above: Day break at trekkers camp on the barren shores of Gokyo's glacial lake, Dudh Pokhari, high in the Himalaya. To the west sunrise lights up the eastern face of the jagged ridge of 18,560 foot high Dragkya Chhulung.

skills and labour remain ridiculously cheap.

In 1984 the minimum legal rate for a guide of the calibre of Sherpa Norgay Tenzing who conquered Everest with Sir Edmund Hilary was fixed at 30 rupees — equivalent to about one dollar — a day.

But the Ministry clearly knows too well the potential of mountain assaults in terms of media coverage and national pride: it keeps a kind of international league table of those national expeditions first to conquer a particular peak.

Of Nepal's 8,000 metre or more summits conquered by 1974, Britain claimed Everest (1953) and Kanchenjunga (1955); France, Annapurna (1950) and Makalu (1955); Japan, Manaslu (1955), Makalu (S.E. Summit) (1970) and Kanchenjunga West (1973); Switzerland, Lhotse (1956) and Dhaulagiri (1960); and Spain, Annapurna South (1974).

Those who climb have many reasons, some inexplicable to people who suffer from vertigo and other neuroses, but among the major delights must be the views. For instance, Annapurna forms part of the natural world's greatest amphitheatre.

From its topmost 26,545 foot high peak in the west, in anti-clockwise direction the climber can look south to Fang (25,089 feet), Moditse Peak (23,683 feet), Hiunchuli (21,133 feet), south-east to Machhapuchhare (22,842 feet) east to Annapurna III (24,787 feet), north-east to Gangapurna (24,457 feet), to Glacier Dome (23,191 feet) and north to Roc Noir (24,556 feet). As if this were not enough, in the middle of this stupendous amphitheatre, truly an arena of the Gods and Goddesses, stand Tent Peak (18,580 feet) and Fluted Peak (21,330 feet).

All this within an inner radius of no more than 40 kilometres!

Its only equal — in scale, form and drama — is directly opposite, across the Kali Gandaki valley, where Dhaulagiri's six peaks, and those around them, form another breathtaking amphitheatre.

To stand at these heights and survey the cloud-wreathed panorama of fluted ice walls, glaciers, hanging ice-cliffs, sheer rock walls and the almost sheer scree approaches, the dangers faced, the hazards overcome, must surely be triumph indeed.

But for the great majority the closest they will come to this ultimate conquest is on foot around the base of the mountains. Thousands spend their Nepal holiday trekking through this tangle of mountains, delighting in the crisp mountain air and camping in alpine meadows, the challenge of negotiating dizzying mountain footpaths with a giddy drop at their feet and crossing over lung-sapping, snow-covered passes at between 15,000 and 19,000 feet: victory enough for those without the skills, time, money or equipment to cling to one of the monstrous walls, traverses or the ridges higher-up, simply 'because they're there'.

All of Nepal is geared up to cater for the high-altitude trekker. In summer — between April and October — the only blemish is the number of leeches which infest the muddy trails. These persistent and loathsome creatures infiltrate everything and the best time to trek is late September and early October when the mountain views are incredible (and continue to be so throughout crisp winter) or in the first quarter of the year when haze tends to cover the peaks.

A risk which the trekker shares with the climber is that of mountain sickness: a combination of nausea, sleeplessness, headaches and potentially lethal oedemas, both cerebral and pulmonary. Sudden ascents to heights of 12,000 feet and more, without acclimatization, lead to accumulations of water on the lungs or brain. Swift descent and prompt medical treatment is the only answer.

Treks around Dhaulagiri take you through a veritable wonderland of meadows, forest and villages among some of the happiest and most generous people in the world, allowing you to savour the simple lifestyles — and delightful scenery — to the full.

The contrast between the stark, ice-white peaks set against the conifer and rhododendron forests, verdant spring and summer fields below, and the azure sky above, can draw your breath as much as climbing these heights.

Villages straggle down the hillsides in a series of terraces, just like the paddy and grain fields, and there's always time and reason enough to rest in one of the many Nepali tea houses, simple little cafes where the refreshment helps beat the debilitating dehydration brought about by altitude and exercise.

Around Dhaulagiri and Annapurna there are dozens of trekking options from which to choose. But around Manaslu Himal there are not so many. All the more delightful perhaps because they're still not beaten tracks and take you to the feet of such giants as 26,760 foot high Manaslu and its sister peaks, including sacred 24,299 foot high Ganesh Himal and its seven lesser peaks and forbidding 25,895 foot high Himal Chuli.

Take the Trisuli Valley through Trisuli Bazaar — also the starting point for treks to neighbouring Langtang Himal — and you'll walk through hills clad with evergreen forests, thundering waterfalls, and alpine plants. Oaks, alders, firs and rhododendrons.

Villages are built of sturdy gabled, two-storey brick and thatch houses. Among the many large and striking monasteries are some which are

Below: Once the bed of an ocean, Mount Everest is now the world's highest point. Where tides ebbed and flowed clouds plume eastward off its 29,028 foot high peak. Formed between 50 and 60 million years ago, Everest and the rest of the 3,500 kilometre long Himalaya mountains have continued to rise, centimetre by centimetre, through the millennia. At right is 25,850 foot high Nuptse and extreme right the raggy peak of 27,890 foot high Lhotse.

Opposite: Steel-hawsered suspension foot bridge crosses the foaming waters born in the Everest region which feed the Dudh Kosi, one of Nepal's major rivers.

Above: Woman at Namche Bazaar, gateway to Sagamartha National Park.

strikingly small: one with pagoda style roofs and a circular top is like a cross between a lighthouse and a Suffolk grain store.

The 14-day trek leaves Ganesh Himal in the east and takes you around the north face of Himal Chuli and Manaslu — almost into China's backyard — through bleak and windswept passes, skirting glaciers and frozen lakes up to a height of more than 15,000 feet.

Close to the border is Somdu, Nepal's most remote permanent settlement, a village of 200 souls — about 40 families — whose fields and paddies are covered with snow until late in the year. There are also the twin villages of Li and Lo to delight lovers of tongue twisters. All along the way the trails are lined with the inevitable prayer stones, *mani* of the staunch Buddhists who occupy the region.

Retracing their footsteps to Trisuli Bazaar, trekkers turn north-east and climb the trail that winds along the east bank of the Trisuli River to enter one of Nepal's most enchanted regions — fabled Langtang Himal with its monasteries, *stupas*, prayer walls and places made sacred by the Hindu scriptures.

Right at the capital's rear door, no city in the world can claim a more incredible backdrop. Tilman called it 'one of the most beautiful valleys in the world': still considered an understatement by some.

Ancient Bo trees, their gnarled limbs like rheumy fingers, spread a thick canopy of shade over Langtang's version of the patio, old stone terraces with seats stepped into the stone work, outside the rustic tea houses which refresh the traveller.

This is the most popular of all Nepal's wilderness areas — a wonderland of hardy mountain people, animals, birds, forests, and mountains — much of it preserved as the nation's second largest national park spread across 1,243 square kilometres. Outside the 20 or so alpine villages roam 30 different species of wildlife while more than 150 different kinds of bird have made their home among the region's 1,000 botanical species.

Mud-and-thatch houses serve as police control posts. As much concern for the welfare of trekkers, as it is good government housekeeping, everybody needs a permit to visit these remote highlands: issued for one destination at a time along prescribed routes.

Dominating the valley at its north end is Nepal's 23,771 foot high Langtang Lirung, a few kilometres beyond which, on the Tibetan border, rises its sister peak, 23,750 foot high Langtang Ri: both overshadowed by Shisha Pangma — sacred 26,398 foot high Gosainthan of Hindu mythology — which lies a few kilometres inside Tibet, one of the legendary abodes of Shiva.

You get sudden and unexpected views of some of these peaks as you take the spectacular trail hacked out of the wall of the gorge above Trisuli. On the more level areas, it cuts through thickets of juniper and rhododendron, blue pine and cushion plants.

For centuries it has been a trade route between Kathmandu and Rasuwa Garhi across the border in Tibet. During July and August this rocky track becomes a mass of humanity: devout Hindu pilgrims, worshippers of Shiva, head for Langtang's Gosainkund lakeland, half a dozen small gems which sparkle in the midday sunshine, said to have been formed when Shiva thrust his trident into the mountainside.

Above: Sherpa mother in the hills around Lukla prepares the family supper: potato pancakes.

Right: Tamang folk dance in mourning during a funeral ceremony at remote village of Bharku in the lovely Langtang Valley. Numbering close to a million, these hardy hill people of Tibeto-Mongoloid descent, are mainly Buddhists.

From Gosainkund it's possible to walk on over the pass into the remote but eternally beautiful reaches of upper Helambu, best in springtime when the rhododendrons bloom. Here too the headwaters of Nepal's major river, the Sun Kosi, mingle together from scores of tumbling waterfalls, roaring rivers and laughing streams.

Swiss explorer, geologist, adventurer Tony Hagen shared Tilman's passion for Langtang Himal and ignited the same feelings in another Swiss — a UN farm advisor — who built a Swiss cheese factory close to Kyangjin monastery at around 14,000 feet which, whatever the quality of the cheese, provides some of the most spectacular mountain views found anywhere.

The people are Tibetan stock from Kyirong who intermarried with Tamangs from Helambu and use a dialect similar to that spoken by the Tibetan community in India's Sikkim area. They cultivate smallholdings for grain and vegetables but are mainly pastoral — herding sheep and yaks.

To western eyes, the yak is one of the oddest looking species of cattle, but well-equipped for its primary role as a high-altitude beef and dairy animal. They thrive in the frosty reaches of the Himalaya, but fare disastrously if translocated to lower regions. They never descend below 14,000 feet and in summer will often reach as high as 20,000 feet.

Long and low, its massive body, which weighs more than 500 kilogrammes, is entirely black with long hair that falls at the sides in sweeping fringes. Its tassled tail makes an ideal fly whisk. Found still in feral communities, many of the domesticated breed are used as pack beasts as well as meat and dairy stock. The domestic hybrid species found at lower altitudes — a cross between a cow and a yak — is smaller.

But Langtang's principal purpose is as a wildlife and botanical reservoir: for the endangered snow leopard, leopard, Himalayan black bear, red panda and wild dog.

These canines differ from the domestic species in that they have fewer teeth and vary in colour acording to their locality. Bigger than jackals, but smaller than wolves, they are found throughout the Himalaya and eastern Tibet.

They are Nepal's most efficient and ruthless killers, running down large deer and sometimes even taking on other predators — there have been instances on the Terai plains where a pack has taken a tiger. Packs vary from six to sixty animals which usually hunt around sunup and sundown.

They kill on the run, ripping out the victim's entrails while it tries to escape. In Nepal, wild dog are found in remote high regions like Langtang as well as on the tropical plains.

The Park's avifauna is equally precious. One hundred and sixty species of birds have been observed in this region including Crested Grebes, Coots, Snow Cocks, Tufted Pochard, Teal, and the Bar-headed Goose as well as game birds like the Blood Pheasant.

Eastward, across the fortress of Langtang Himal's peaks, lies the Rolwaling Himal, that little-known and overshadowed annexe of the great Everest massif. Accessible with ease only from the west, it is considered as beautiful as Langtang. At the far end of the Bhotey Kosi gorge, 23,560 foot high Menlungtse and the slightly lower 23,442 foot

Above: Lama of the Tamang village monastery at Syabru in the Langtang Valley north of Kathmandu Valley.

high mass of Gaurisankar stand sentinel, like Lhotse and Nuptse, guarding Sagamartha, Everest, hiding her massive pyramid from prying and curious eyes.

Though almost 6,000 feet lower than Everest, Guarisankar is truly majestic: in the form of an amphitheatre, its back faces north-west, and where the evening sun casts its glow over the curve of the shoulders it paints its sheer ice cliff in soft gold. Surely, it's easy to believe that Shiva and his consort still live here, where the wind plays ancient anthems in the crevasses and cracks, singing songs of praise to faiths older than mankind's, and spindrift raises a plume of white that plays across the mountain's brow, shaping the destiny of their legion of followers below.

High up the valley, perched on top of a line of cliffs, the hide-out of long-tailed grey langurs, is Simigaon, a hamlet built by a community of Sherpas and Tamangs. Above, the trail reaches the saddle of Sambur Danda and — suddenly, breathtakingly — spread out before you is Gaurisankar, sweeping up in serrated, jagged ridges and layers to its twin summits.

Here, beyond the tree-line where the land is stark and bare, scree and rocks scattered down from the snowy heights above in mounds and ridges, the sense of the supernatural sharpens. Allusion and illusion begin to assume solid shape.

Particularly that creature of fable and myth — 'the Abominable Snowman', *yeti*. Though there is not a single zoological specimen nor any proof of its existence, in 1964 King Mahendra's Government promulgated a law banning the hunting of this legendary creature said to come in three different shapes and sizes according to which story-teller is relating its shaggy-haired adventures.

In one form it's a huge two and a half metre tall cattle eater, usually seen on all fours. In another it's a small ape-like beast with gangling arms and red or blond body hair. In the definitive form it's man-sized, covered in red shaggy hair except on the face and stomach, and walks upright. It is said to attack on sight, devouring even human beings.

Stories of this wild half-man, half-beast were heard in the west more than five centuries ago — from a European mercenary who served in Mongolia. More recently, in 1899, Major L.A. Waddell, investigating marks in the snow described the mysterious footprints which he had found in the Himalaya.

Twenty two years later, surveying Everest's north face from Tibet, Colonel C.K. Howard-Bury saw strange creatures moving across the mountain's snow slopes and later came across enormous footprints.

Footprints similar to those photographed by Eric Shipton on a late afternoon in November 1951 on the Menlungtse Glacier which frowns down on Rolwaling Valley. With Sherpa Sen Tenzing, Shipton followed the footprints across the snow for more than a mile before the snow gave way to moraine scree. His photographs, clear and sharp, show a very wide oval footprint with a very prominent protruding big toe.

This so intrigued the western world that a series of expeditions determined to uncover the *yeti*. Britain's *Daily Mail* despatched an impressive team of experts in 1954 and in the following years a Texas millionaire mounted a series of expeditions.

The elusive beast escaped them. But like the Loch Ness Monster, the

Above: Rock terraces hold stony but precious soil of Khumjung's potato farms. Perched 12,500 feet high on the slopes of Khumbila, about two hours walk from Namche Bazaar, the local monastery has for years zealously guarded the alleged scalp of a yeti, the mysterious 'Abominable Snowman'. A rock-hard dome covered with red bristles it was declared the hide of a Himalayan goat after laboratory analysis in America.

yeti will never die. In 1958 interest was sparked anew by a climber's discovery of the same kind of footprints Shipton had photographed.

By 1960 Sir Edmund Hilary, conqueror of Everest, was in the Rolwaling Valley with an expedition loaded with scientific equipment determined to establish the truth — but with strict orders from the Nepalese Government not to kill or capture the creature.

Yeti furs found by the expedition turned out be from the carcasses of Tibetan blue bears. A sacred relic — said to be a *yeti* scalp — was taken from its 200 year old keeping place in Khumjung Monastery and examined in America and Europe where it was analysed as being made from the hide of the serow, one of the feral goat species of the Himalaya.

Yet the *yeti* legend persists. Fourteen years later a Sherpa girl told of how she had been attacked by a *yeti*. The bodies of several yaks were found — their necks broken by some terrible force which had taken hold of their horns and twisted their heads.

The same year — and again in 1980 — climbers in the Himalaya woke up in the morning to find strange footprints in the snow outside their camps. Those that trailed after them heard distant screams as if warning them off.

Fancy can play many tricks, particularly amid the rarefied air of the lonely peaks but footprints in the snow, found so often at such irregular intervals, would seem to have more substance than simply a fevered imagination.

The *yeti* may well yet be found to exist — perhaps in the lonely little-visited reaches of the Rolwaling Valley.

Its twin citadels of Gaurisankar and Menlungtse are the westernmost bastions of the Everest massif. Peak to peak a distance of about 70 kilometres separates Shiva's abode from that of Sagamartha, Goddess of the Universe. In between, and around and about, are literally dozens of

184

Left: Three generations of Sherpa women in the mountain ranges around Everest.

lesser ramparts extending to the central pinnacle, most rising above 20,000 feet.

Thirty kilometres distant from Everest, 26,750 foot high Cho Oyu guards the north-west approach while, fewer than eight kilometres distant from the pinnacle of the world, 27,890 foot high Lhotse guards the eastern flank and 25,850 foot high Nuptse the south-western flank. Sixteen kilometres beyond Lhotse, 27,802 foot high Makalu and its four other peaks barricade the approach from the south-east.

Thus, well-guarded, from the ground or the air, Everest hides herself, almost demurely, behind her cluster of courtier peaks with Nuptse and Lhotse serving as ladies-in-waiting.

Yet the mountain's perfect apex, befitting the highest point on earth, was surely designed to be seen. In the foreground, the attendant spires form jagged needles in the sea of cloud which covers the outer slopes. The jet streams keep a constant plume flowing eastwards off the 29,028 foot high summit.

Like the sea from which they rose, these mountains make waves. Aboard the Royal Nepal Airlines daily mountain flight, Captain R.B. Shrestha who has flown the Himalaya daily for seven years and still finds it a tremendous and exhilarating experience, explains.

'You can feel already that it's a little bumpy,' he says in April. 'When the monsoons start, then we get the mountain waves.' These are tremendous thermal breakers in the sky, successive wave upon wave of alternating hot and cold air.

'We can't fly then. The plane pitches up and down just as if you were in a storm-tossed ocean.'

The simile works. You feel you could almost reach out and touch the peaks streaming by on the starboard side of the four-engined Avro. But no words can adequately describe the landscape and its impact — rank upon rank of peaks marching upwards, like a frosty staircase barnacled with icicles, all the way up to the top and down the other side to the Tibetan plateau which lies at around 15,000 to 18,000 feet.

The scenery is cataclysmic. The thrusting jagged spires, knife-edge ridges and glaciers with their surface churned as if by a marching army, deadly pitfalls beneath for the unwary, thrust away into infinity. Numbur, 22,800 feet high, is the pinnacle of a great east-facing amphitheatre, the morning sun scintillating on its snows, a plume of spindrift gusting from the top.

'No matter how many times you fly along here,' says Captain Shrestha, 'it's still a surprise. It always takes your breath away.' Royal Nepal Airlines flies — often in some of the worst possible weather conditions in the world — to perhaps the most inaccessible airfields in the world. In a roadless land they are often the only link between one small community and another, flying an assortment of single-engined, high-winged 10-seater capacity planes, twin-engined planes, and Fokker-Friendships, through narrow mountain defiles often wreathed in cloud to landing strips that stand as high as 14,000 feet.

But people still prefer to travel by air no matter the peril. It's easy to understand why. By foot from the nearest road it takes anything from 12 to 15 days, for instance, to reach Namche Bazaar, the launching point for assaults on Everest or treks along the narrow valleys beneath it.

By plane however it is only 40 minutes from Kathmandu to Lukla, just over 9,000 feet above sea level with a landing strip that's on an uphill gradient and where one side drops precipitously thousands of feet to the floor of the Dudh Kosi Valley.

Namche Bazaar is well above Lukla. But there's also a 13,000 foot airfield nearby — at Shangboche where guests of the Everest View Hotel, with oxygen in all the bedrooms, alight.

Almost everybody who visits Nepal dreams of standing at the foot of the world's greatest mountain but it's an achievement only for the fittest. Most of the trail takes you above 13,000 feet in thin, freezing, raw air — chest pounding, lungs gasping — to 20,000 foot high Everest base camp, higher than any point in Africa or Europe.

Above: Smiling Sherpa children with a friendly welcome for passers-by on the trail from Lukla to Namche Bazaar.

Above: Venerable Lama of Thyangboche Monastery which at 12,710 feet stands in the shadows of Everest. The Lama, a reincarnation of a previous spiritual leader born the instant his predecessor died, was invested at the age of 5 years after rituals confirmed his right to the office.

Yet it's not just the mountain and its huddle of neighbouring peaks, three of the world's seven highest, which is the sole attraction, for this is also a land of fable and monastery, remote meadows, wildlife and the home of the hardy Sherpa folk and their colourful culture.

The trail from Lukla climbs up the Dudh Kosi canyon, zig-zagging from side to side through stone-walled fields, rustic villages and hardy forests. The Buddhist prayer — *Om mani padme hum,* Hail to the jewel in the Lotus — is carved everywhere, on stone walls and the huge boulders which stand by the side of the trail.

Before Namche Bazaar, at the village of Josare, lies the headquarters of Sagamartha National Park where rangers and wardens, used to high-altitude living, relax at 13,000 feet with games like volleyball!

More than 5,000 trekkers a year climb this trail to enter the National Park's 1,243 square kilometres of mountain wilderness: the rumpled brown-green buttresses of Everest ascending ever higher as you climb upward.

Each step becomes an exercise in foot-dragging exhaustion. At your side, a 5,000 foot drop. In your head, a splitting pain. In your stomach, nausea. On your feet, blisters. In your eyes, water. 'Lie down, lie down', your body commands. But no. This is the Abode of the Gods, not to be seen faintly, from a distance. Draw near and be mesmerised. Suddenly, on a ridge the cloud clears and there is Sagamartha, so huge and brooding it seems as if it is about to thunder down on top of you. Thousands yearn to climb its side, many have died in the striving.

Next morning, when you wake in Namche Bazaar, the pain has gone: only sore feet remind you of the challenge ahead, here among the lofty summits and flowing glaciers, plunging waterfalls and snow-fed rivers.

The town, capital of the Sherpa community, is set on a small plateau at the foot of sacred 18,901 foot high Khumbila which staunches the long run of the Ngojumba Glacier that slides down from the base of Cho Oyu. It is the focal point of everything that occurs in the Everest region.

Every Saturday morning there's a colourful market when hundreds trek in from the surrounding villages and towns to haggle and argue, buying and selling. Namche's streets step up the barren, rocky slopes of Khumbila lined with pleasant white-washed two-storey homes and shingle and tin roofs.

Of Mongolian stock, the Sherpa people migrated over the Himalaya centuries ago from Minyak in eastern Tibet. Numbering between 25,000 and 30,000 they're known the world over because it was Sherpa Norgay Tenzing, with Sir Edmund Hilary, who conquered Everest: and it's the Sherpas who accompany every major expedition. For hardihood, courage and endurance there are few to equal these stocky, ever-cheerful uncomplaining folk.

Their dialect is based on the Tibetan language and although they have earned their international reputation as the world's greatest climbers only since 1950, for centuries they have traded, tilled their fragile mountain soils and herded their yaks.

Tucked away in their once-remote mountain fastness, religion still plays a large part in their lives, their daily routines shaped around the inspiration of their Buddhist faith.

It was A.M. Kellas who first used Sherpas in a mountain assault in

1907 in Sikkim. But their real advance came with the opening of the Nepal Himalaya in 1950s: so courageous and skilful were they on the perilous slopes of these giants that the Alpine Club gave them the title, 'Tigers of the Snow'.

Sherpa Tenzing earned immortality from his ascent with Hilary but he died in lonely poverty in exile in Delhi, India, in 1986. Others of his kin have since followed him to the top of the world. One, Pertemba Sherpa, has been there twice. Their high-altitude environment prepares them physically and mentally for the challenges of climbing 29,000 feet into the sky.

Since they were swept before the invading Mongol hordes seven or eight hundred years ago, they have maintained much of their nomadic life style: in summer moving up to the sparse pastures above 19,000 feet. In the past, they migrated to Tibet in summer, returning to winter in the Khumbu region. Slowly, tilling fields and growing vegetables like the potato, they settled in more permanent communities.

Made up of 18 clans — each speaking its own dialect — traditionally some clans cannot marry into another. Tribal law also prohibits members of the same clan from marrying. Gifts of the Sherpa home-brewed beer, *chhang*, are exchanged between heads of families when offspring become engaged. Weddings are elaborate and lavish affairs with great feasting and drinking.

The big men in society are the traders and money-lenders. Usury is big business in hard-up Khumbu with loans at 25 to 30 per cent interest not uncommon.

Yaks provide butter for the lamps which burn in the monasteries and private homes and for the rancid Tibetan tea served in these parts.

Art and handicrafts are limited but images, scrolls, murals, and rock carving provide lucrative reward for Sherpa priests, *lamas* who have become skilled artists. They belong to the oldest Buddhist sect in Tibet, still largely unreformed.

The priests have borrowed freely from the arts of sorcery and witchcraft to sustain their authority and sacrifice is a ritualistic tool to deal with the mythological demons and gods which inhabit every peak and recess of the region and whose presence is confirmed in the Buddhist scriptures of the Sherpas.

Sherpa monasteries, reflecting their Tibetan heritage, are the most striking in Nepal. You'll find them in the towns of Kunde and Khumjung which stand above Namche Bazaar — and are well worth visiting if you can make the climb — on the slopes of of Khumbila.

West of Namche, at the foot of the Bhotey Kosi Valley which is fed by the Jasamba Glacier, there's a particularly striking monastery in the village of Thami.

You can use Namche to approach Cho Oyu, either west up the Bhote Kosi Valley or north of Khumbila up the Dudh Kosi Valley. If you take the westward route you'll climb the Renjo Pass, coming down to Dudh Pokari, a beautiful glacial lake in the Ngojumba Glacier. There's a passable chance *en route* of seeing some of Sagamartha National Park's wildlife: wolf, bear, musk deer, feral goat species and maybe the brilliantly coloured Crimson-horned or Impeyan pheasants of this region.

Above: Intricately worked prayer wheels at Thyangboche Monastery, high in the Himalaya, close to Mount Everest. Within each wheel are hundreds of folded prayer papers.

Right: Ornate painting in Himalayan Monastery. These works of art are usually performed by the lamas who travel long distances to produce such rich and vibrant murals. Rewards are higher than most among the mountain communities.

On the trail to Everest, a hard four-hour slog, or a full day's strenuous effort from Namche, you'll come to the best known of Khumbu's monasteries, Thyangboche, known the world over from photographs with stupendous views of Everest, or maybe Lhotse or the unmistakeable 22,494 foot high obelisk of Ama Dablam, in the background.

Since his successful ascent of Everest on 29 May 1953 Sir Edmund Hilary has become New Zealand's Ambassador to India and Nepal and devoted much of his diplomatic career and his personal life to improving life for the Sherpa community which he has come to love. He is a frequent visitor to the Monastery and the *lama* who presides.

It was his initiative which led to the establishment of Sagamartha National Park in 1975 which was run by New Zealand experts until 1981 when Nepal took over its management. Hilary has been back frequently, helping to build schools and community centres. Civilizing forces, not all for the better, have come apace to the once-isolated Sherpas whose festivals add colour and fantasy to life in this barren but beautiful region.

Above: Sir Edmund Hilary, conqueror of Everest with Sherpa Tenzing in May 1953, joyously accepts the gift of a white shawl, khada, *from young Sherpa novice monks at Thyangboche Monastery during a 1986 visit. The white shawl is mandatory garb if visitors wish to meet the Lama.*

The first major assault on Everest took place in 1924 when George Mallory and Andrew Irvine disappeared on the mountain close to the summit. Their bodies still lie somewhere beneath Sagamartha's eternal snows. They took a route along the north-east ridge from Tibet. Mystery still surrounds their disappearance: some believe they may have actually reached the summit and in 1986 the American mountaineer Tom Holzel led an expedition to ascertain the truth and search for Mallory's body. Others followed their fatal — and difficult — route.

It was only when Nepal opened its borders that the south face, the line taken by Hilary and Tenzing, was approachable. Standing atop the world, Hilary said, profanely: 'We've done the bitch.'

Since it was first surveyed as a climbing challenge by Mallory in 1921, the mountain has punished many of those who challenged it, claiming a total of more than 60 lives.

More than 70 groups from 21 nations have taken part in expeditions and 149 people, four of them women, have stood where Hilary and Tenzing first stood — one, a Japanese called Yuichiro Miura, descending more than six thousand feet from a height of about 26,000 feet on skis at a speed around 150 kilometres an hour. But this feat cost the lives of six Sherpas accompanying the expedition who were swept away in an avalanche. The first woman, Mrs Junko Tabai, also a Japanese, conquered Everest on 16 May 1975.

But even after reaching the summit, the euphoria of looking out from the highest point on earth, an exultant moment, is no cause to relax. The descent is as perilous as the climb upwards. Yasuo Kata, the first person to climb it in three different seasons — spring, autumn and winter — experienced that exultation for the third time in 1982 but never lived to tell of it. He died in a storm making his way back down the mountain.

For years it was thought no man could climb to such heights without oxygen but Austrian Peter Habeler and Italian Reinhold Messner achieved the feat in 1978 and two years later, unquestionably the greatest climber the world has known, Messner repeated the feat in a solo climb, this time from Tibet along the north-east ridge, which claimed Mallory and Irvine.

He first established a base camp in mid-July at 21,400 feet. After weeks of acclimatisation, he set out in the darkness of the Tibetan sky at 0500 hours on 18 August 1980 — reaching the summit above a bank of black storm clouds at 1520 on 20 August to spend 40 minutes there before returning.

Despite the loss of his brother during an assault on Pakistan's Nanga Parbat in 1970 — one of his earliest Himalayan challenges — and most of his toes from frostbite, Messner is driven to climb, as if by some mystical compulsion, in lonely solitude.

During his solo assault on Everest he experienced wind gusts of more than 80 kilometres an hour. He recalls reaching the summit. 'I sat there like a stone. I had spent every bit of strength to get there...I still do not know how I managed to achieve the summit. I only know that I couldn't have gone on any longer...I don't think I could handle it again. I was at my limit.'

Yet as long as Sagamartha stands above the jet streams so will there be men to challenge her.

Indeed, Messner in 1986 achieved his ambition to climb all 14 of the world's great mountains, including the third highest peak in the world, Kanchenjunga, on Nepal's border with Sikkim, which he saw — 'far to the east...protruding above a blanket of clouds, a majestic sight' — from the saddle of the North Col on Everest during the first day of his climb.

Leaving the shadows of the brave and foolish who still lie on Sagamartha's slopes — including an English religious zealot without any mountain experience who fell to his death in the 1930s after leaving behind in his diary the epitaph: 'Off again. Gorgeous day' — Messner would have travelled 125 kilometres eastward from Everest as the crow flies to stand atop 28,208 foot high Kanchenjunga astride Nepal's border with India's Sikkim State.

Here too is a massif of giant peaks — 15 of them above 23,000 feet — and looking westward on a clear day Nepal in all its diversity stretches out before you in infinity as if it will never end, from the steamy Terai Plains, through its midland mountains and valleys, up to the Himalaya, the 'Roof of the World'.

Too marvellous by far to be anything but a dream, the astonishing thing is that it exists. If it did not, however, be sure: nobody could ever have invented a country so fabulous.

Indeed, alone beneath Kanchenjunga's mighty peak on a moonlit night, the mountain snows soft and luminous, the stars pin-sharp, Kipling might well have written:

> *Still the world is wondrous large —*
> *seven seas from marge to marge —*
> *and it holds a vast of various kinds of man*
> *And the greatest wonders of this world*
> *by nature are here unfurled*